Veloce *Classic Reprint* Series

Saab

96 & V4

Also from Veloce Publishing:

Those Were The Days ... Series
Alpine Trials & Rallies 1910-1973 (Pfundner)
American 'Independent' Automakers – AMC to Willys 1945 to 1960 (Mort)
American Station Wagons – The Golden Era 1950-1975 (Mort)
American Trucks of the 1950s (Mort)
American Trucks of the 1960s (Mort)
American Woodies 1928-1953 (Mort)
Anglo-American Cars from the 1930s to the 1970s (Mort)
Austerity Motoring (Bobbitt)
Austins, The last real (Peck)
Brighton National Speed Trials (Gardiner)
British and European Trucks of the 1970s (Peck)
British Drag Racing – The early years (Pettitt)
British Lorries of the 1950s (Bobbitt)
British Lorries of the 1960s (Bobbitt)
British Touring Car Racing (Collins)
British Police Cars (Walker)
British Woodies (Peck)
Café Racer Phenomenon, The (Walker)
Don Hayter's MGB Story – The birth of the MGB in MG's Abingdon Design & Development Office (Hayter)
Drag Bike Racing in Britain – From the mid '60s to the mid '80s (Lee)
Dune Buggy Phenomenon, The (Hale)
Dune Buggy Phenomenon Volume 2, The (Hale)
Endurance Racing at Silverstone in the 1970s & 1980s (Parker)
Hot Rod & Stock Car Racing in Britain in the 1980s (Neil)
Mercedes-Benz Trucks (Peck)
MG's Abingdon Factory (Moylan)
Motor Racing at Brands Hatch in the Seventies (Parker)
Motor Racing at Brands Hatch in the Eighties (Parker)
Motor Racing at Crystal Palace (Collins)
Motor Racing at Goodwood in the Sixties (Gardiner)
Motor Racing at Nassau in the 1950s & 1960s (O'Neil)
Motor Racing at Oulton Park in the 1960s (McFadyen)
Motor Racing at Oulton Park in the 1970s (McFadyen)
Motor Racing at Thruxton in the 1970s (Grant-Braham)
Motor Racing at Thruxton in the 1980s (Grant-Braham)
Superprix – The Story of Birmingham Motor Race (Page & Collins)
Three Wheelers (Bobbitt)

Great Cars
Austin-Healey – A celebration of the fabulous 'Big' Healey (Piggott)
Jaguar E-type (Thorley)
Jaguar Mark 1 & 2 (Thorley)
Triumph TR – TR2 to 6: The last of the traditional sports cars (Piggott)

Rally Giants Series
Audi Quattro (Robson)
Austin Healey 100-6 & 3000 (Robson)
Fiat 131 Abarth (Robson)
Ford Escort MkI (Robson)
Ford Escort RS Cosworth & World Rally Car (Robson)
Ford Escort RS1800 (Robson)
Lancia Delta 4WD/Integrale (Robson)
Lancia Stratos (Robson)
Mini Cooper/Mini Cooper S (Robson)
Peugeot 205 T16 (Robson)
Saab 96 & V4 (Robson)
Subaru Impreza (Robson)
Toyota Celica GT4 (Robson)

WSC Giants
Audi R8 (Wagstaff)
Ferrari 312P & 312PB (Collins & McDonough)
Gulf-Mirage 1967 to 1982 (McDonough)
Matra Sports Cars – MS620, 630, 650, 660 & 670 – 1966 to 1974 (McDonough)

Biographies
A Chequered Life – Graham Warner and the Chequered Flag (Hesletine)
A Life Awheel – The 'auto' biography of W de Forte (Skelton)
Amédée Gordini ... a true racing legend (Smith)
André Lefebvre, and the cars he created at Voisin and Citroën (Beck)
Chris Carter at Large – Stories from a lifetime in motorcycle racing (Carter & Skelton)
Cliff Allison, The Official Biography of – From the Fells to Ferrari (Gauld)
Edward Turner – The Man Behind the Motorcycles (Clew)
Driven by Desire – The Desiré Wilson Story
First Principles – The Official Biography of Keith Duckworth (Burr)
Inspired to Design – F1 cars, Indycars & racing tyres: the autobiography of Nigel Bennett (Bennett)
Jack Sears, The Official Biography of – Gentleman Jack (Gauld)
Jim Redman – 6 Times World Motorcycle Champion: The Autobiography (Redman)
John Chatham – 'Mr Big Healey' – The Official Biography (Burr)
The Lee Noble Story (Wilkins)
Mason's Motoring Mayhem – Tony Mason's hectic life in motorsport and television (Mason)
Raymond Mays' Magnificent Obsession (Apps)
Pat Moss Carlsson Story, The – Harnessing Horsepower (Turner)
'Sox' – Gary Hocking – the forgotten World Motorcycle Champion (Hughes)
Tony Robinson – The biography of a race mechanic (Wagstaff)
Virgil Exner – Visioneer: The Official Biography of Virgil M Exner Designer Extraordinaire (Grist)

General
1½-litre GP Racing 1961-1965 (Whitelock)
AC Two-litre Saloons & Buckland Sportscars (Archibald)
Alpine & Renault – The Development of the Revolutionary Turbo F1 Car 1968 to 1979 (Smith)
Alpine & Renault – The Sports Prototypes 1963 to 1969 (Smith)
Alpine & Renault – The Sports Prototypes 1973 to 1978 (Smith)
An Austin Anthology (Stringer)
An Incredible Journey (Falls & Reisch)
Anatomy of the Classic Mini (Huthert & Ely)
Anatomy of the Works Minis (Moylan)
Austin Cars 1948 to 1990 – a pictorial history (Rowe)
Autodrome (Collins & Ireland)
Automotive A-Z, Lane's Dictionary of Automotive Terms (Lane)
Automotive Mascots (Kay & Springate)
Bahamas Speed Weeks, The (O'Neil)
Bluebird CN7 (Stevens)
BMC Competitions Department Secrets (Turner, Chambers & Browning)
British at Indianapolis, The (Wagstaff)
British Café Racers (Cloesen)
British Cars, The Complete Catalogue of, 1895-1975 (Culshaw & Horrobin)
British Custom Motorcycles – The Brit Chop – choppers, cruisers, bobbers & trikes (Cloesen)
BRM – A Mechanic's Tale (Salmon)
BRM V16 (Ludvigsen)
BSA Bantam Bible, The (Henshaw)
BSA Motorcycles – the final evolution (Jones)
Carrera Panamericana, La (Tipler)
Car-tastrophes – 80 automotive atrocities from the past 20 years (Honest John, Fowler)
Chrysler 300 – America's Most Powerful Car 2nd Edition (Ackerson)
Chrysler PT Cruiser (Ackerson)
Citroën DS (Bobbitt)
Classic British Car Electrical Systems (Astley)
Cobra – The Real Thing! (Legate)
Competition Car Aerodynamics 3rd Edition (McBeath)
Competition Car Composites A Practical Handbook (Revised 2nd Edition) (McBeath)
Concept Cars, How to illustrate and design – New 2nd Edition (Dewey)
Cortina – Ford's Bestseller (Robson)
Cosworth – The Search for Power (6th edition) (Robson)
Coventry Climax Racing Engines (Hammill)
Daily Mirror 1970 World Cup Rally 40, The (Robson)
Drive on the Wild Side, A – 20 Extreme Driving Adventures From Around the World (Weaver)
East German Motor Vehicles in Pictures (Suhr/Weinreich)
Essential Guide to Driving in Europe, The (Parish)
Fast Ladies – Female Racing Drivers 1888 to 1970 (Bouzanquet)
Fate of the Sleeping Beauties, The (op de Weegh/Hottendorff/op de Weegh)
Ferrari 288 GTO, The Book of the (Sackey)
Ferrari 333 SP (O'Neil)
Fiat & Abarth 124 Spider & Coupé (Tipler)
Fiat & Abarth 500 & 600 – 2nd Edition (Bobbitt)
Fiats, Great Small (Ward)
Ford Cleveland 335-Series V8 engine 1970 to 1982 – The Essential Source Book (Hammill)
Ford F100/F150 Pick-up 1948-1996 (Ackerson)
Ford F150 Pick-up 1997-2005 (Ackerson)
Ford Focus WRC (Robson)
Ford GT – Then, and Now (Streather)
Ford GT40 (Legate)
Ford Midsize Muscle – Fairlane, Torino & Ranchero (Cranswick)
Ford Model Y (Roberts)
Ford Small Block V8 Racing Engines 1962-1970 – The Essential Source Book (Hammill)
Formula One – The Real Score? (Harvey)
Formula 5000 Motor Racing, Back then ... and back now (Lawson)
Forza Minardi! (Vigar)
The Good, the Mad and the Ugly ... not to mention Jeremy Clarkson (Dron)
Grand Prix Ferrari – The Years of Enzo Ferrari's Power, 1948-1980 (Pritchard)
Grand Prix Ford – DFV-powered Formula 1 Cars (Robson)
GT – The World's Best GT Cars 1953-73 (Dawson)
Hillclimbing & Sprinting – The Essential Manual (Short & Wilkinson)
Honda NSX (Long)
Immortal Austin Seven (Morgan)
Karmann-Ghia Coupé & Convertible (Bobbitt)
Kawasaki Triples Bible, The (Walker)
Kris Meeke – Intercontinental Rally Challenge Champion (McBride)
Lancia 037 (Collins)
Lancia Delta HF Integrale (Blaettel & Wagner)
Lancia Delta Integrale (Collins)
Le Mans Panoramic (Ireland)
Lexus Story, The (Long)
Maserati 250F In Focus (Pritchard)
Maximum Mini (Booij)
Mercedes G-Wagen (Long)
MG, Made in Abingdon (Frampton)
MGA (Price Williams)
MGB & MGB GT– Expert Guide (Auto-doc Series) (Williams)
MGB Electrical Systems Updated & Revised Edition (Astley)
Micro Trucks (Mort)
Microcars at Large! (Quellin)
Mini Cooper – The Real Thing! (Tipler)
Mini Minor to Asia Minor (West)
Mitsubishi Lancer Evo, The Road Car & WRC Story (Long)
Montlhéry, The Story of the Paris Autodrome (Boddy)
MOPAR Muscle – Barracuda, Dart & Valiant 1960-1980 (Cranswick)
Morgan Maverick (Lawrence)
Morgan 3 Wheeler – back to the future!, The (Dron)
Morris Minor, 70 Years on the Road (Newell)
Motor Racing – Reflections of a Lost Era (Carter)
Motor Racing – The Pursuit of Victory 1930-1962 (Carter)
Motor Racing – The Pursuit of Victory 1963-1972 (Wyatt/Sears)
Motor Racing Heroes – The Stories of 100 Greats (Newman)
Motorcycle Apprentice (Cakebread)
Motorcycle GP Racing in the 1960s (Pereira)
Motorcycle Racing with the Continental Circus 1920-1970 (Pereira)
Motorcycle Road & Racing Chassis Designs (Noakes)
Motorcycling in the '50s (Clew)
Motorhomes, The Illustrated History (Jenkinson)
Motorsport In colour, 1950s (Wainwright)
MV Agusta Fours, The book of the classic (Falloon)
N.A.R.T. – A concise history of the North American Racing Team 1957 to 1983 (O'Neil)
Nissan 300ZX & 350Z – The Z-Car Story (Long)
Nissan GT-R Supercar: Born to race (Gorodji)
Northeast American Sports Car Races 1950-1959 (O'Neil)
Norton Commando Bible – All models 1968 to 1978 (Henshaw)
Nothing Runs – Misadventures in the Classic, Collectable & Exotic Car Biz (Slutsky)
Off-Road Giants! (Volume 1) – Heroes of 1960s Motorcycle Sport (Westlake)
Off-Road Giants! (Volume 2) – Heroes of 1960s Motorcycle Sport (Westlake)
Off-Road Giants! (Volume 3) – Heroes of 1960s Motorcycle Sport (Westlake)
Pass the Theory and Practical Driving Tests (Gibson & Hoole)
Peking to Paris 2007 (Young)
Pontiac Firebird – New 3rd Edition (Cranswick)
Preston Tucker & Others (Linde)
RAC Rally Action! (Gardiner)
Racing Colours – Motor Racing Compositions 1908-2009 (Newman)
Racing Line – British motorcycle racing in the golden age of the big single (Guntrip)
Rallye Sport Fords: The Inside Story (Moreton)
The Red Baron's Ultimate Ducati Desmo Manual (Cabrera Choclán)
Renewable Energy Home Handbook, The (Porter)
Roads with a View – England's greatest views and how to find them by road (Corfield)
Rolls-Royce Silver Shadow/Bentley T Series Corniche & Camargue – Revised & Enlarged Edition (Bobbitt)
Rolls-Royce Silver Spirit, Silver Spur & Bentley Mulsanne 2nd Edition (Bobbitt)
Rootes Cars of the 50s, 60s & 70s – Hillman, Humber, Singer, Sunbeam & Talbot (Rowe)
Rover P4 (Bobbitt)
Runways & Racers (O'Neil)
Russian Motor Vehicles – Soviet Limousines 1930-2003 (Kelly)
Russian Motor Vehicles – The Czarist Period 1784 to 1917 (Kelly)
RX-7 – Mazda's Rotary Engine Sportscar (Updated & Revised New Edition) (Long)
Scooters & Microcars, The A-Z of Popular (Dan)
Scooter Lifestyle (Grainger)
Scooter Mania! – Recollections of the Isle of Man International Scooter Rally (Jackson)
Singer Story: Cars, Commercial Vehicles, Bicycles & Motorcycle (Atkinson)
Sleeping Beauties USA – abandoned classic cars & trucks (Marek)
SM – Citroën's Maserati-engined Supercar (Long & Claverol)
Speedway – Auto racing's ghost tracks (Collins & Ireland)
Sprite Caravans, The Story of (Jenkinson)
Standard Motor Company, The Book of the (Robson)
Steve Hole's Kit Car Cornucopia – Cars, Companies, Stories, Facts & Figures: the UK's kit car scene since 1949 (Hole)
Subaru Impreza: The Road Car And WRC Story (Long)
Supercar, How to Build your own (Thompson)
Tales from the Toolbox (Oliver)
Tatra – The Legacy of Hans Ledwinka, Updated & Enlarged Collector's Edition of 1500 copies (Margolius & Henry)
Taxi! The Story of the 'London' Taxicab (Bobbitt)
This Day in Automotive History (Corey)
To Boldly Go – twenty six vehicle designs that dared to be different (Hull)
Toleman Story, The (Hilton)
Toyota Celica & Supra, The Book of Toyota's Sports Coupés (Long)
Toyota MR2 Coupés & Spyders (Long)
Triumph & Standard Cars 1945 to 1984 (Warrington)
Triumph Bonneville Bible (59-83) (Henshaw)
Triumph Bonneville!, Save the – The inside story of the Meriden Workers' Co-op (Rosamond)
Triumph Motorcycles & the Meriden Factory (Hancox)
Triumph Speed Twin & Thunderbird Bible (Woolridge)
Triumph Tiger Cub Bible (Estall)
Triumph Trophy Bible (Woolridge)
Triumph TR6 (Kimberley)
TT Talking – The TT's most exciting era – As seen by Manx Radio TT's lead commentator 2004-2012 (Lambert)
Two Summers – The Mercedes-Benz W196R Racing Car (Ackerson)
TWR Story, The – Group A (Hughes & Scott)
Unraced (Collins)
Velocette Motorcycles – MSS to Thruxton – Third Edition (Burris)
Vespa – The Story of a Cult Classic in Pictures (Uhlig)
Vincent Motorcycles: The Untold Story since 1946 (Guyony & Parker)
Volkswagen Bus Book, The (Bobbitt)
Volkswagen Bus or Van to Camper, How to Convert (Porter)
Volkswagens of the World (Glen)
VW Beetle Cabriolet – The full story of the convertible Beetle (Bobbitt)
VW Beetle – The Car of the 20th Century (Copping)
VW Bus – 40 Years of Splitties, Bays & Wedges (Copping)
VW Bus Book, The (Bobbitt)
VW Golf: Five Generations of Fun (Copping & Cservenka)
VW – The Air-cooled Era (Copping)
VW T5 Camper Conversion Manual (Porter)
VW Campers (Copping)
Volkswagen Type 3, The book of the – Concept, Design, International Production Models & Development (Glen)
Volvo Estate, The (Hollebone)
You & Your Jaguar XK8/XKR – Buying, Enjoying, Maintaining, Modifying – New Edition (Thorley)
Which Oil? – Choosing the right oils & greases for your antique, vintage, veteran, classic or collector car (Michell)
Wolseley Cars 1948 to 1975 (Rowe)
Works Minis, The Last (Purves & Brenchley)
Works Rally Mechanic (Moylan)

www.veloce.co.uk

First published under ISBN 978-1-845842-56-7 in April 2010 by Veloce Publishing Limited, Veloce House, Parkway Farm Business Park, Middle Farm Way, Poundbury, Dorchester DT1 3AR, England. Fax 01305 250479/Tel 01305 260068/e-mail info@veloce.co.uk/web www.veloce.co.uk or www.velocebooks.com.
Veloce Classic Reprint edition printed April 2018.
ISBN 978-1-787113-32-9. UPC 6-36847-01332-5

© Graham Robson and Veloce Publishing 2010 & 2018. All rights reserved. With the exception of quoting brief passages for the purpose of review, no part of this publication may be recorded, reproduced or transmitted by any means, including photocopying, without the written permission of Veloce Publishing Ltd. Throughout this book logos, model names and designations, etc, have been used for the purposes of identification, illustration and decoration. Such names are the property of the trademark holder as this is not an official publication.

Readers with ideas for automotive books, or books on other transport or related hobby subjects, are invited to write to the editorial director of Veloce Publishing at the above address.
British Library Cataloguing in Publication Data – A catalogue record for this book is available from the British Library. Typesetting, design and page make-up all by Veloce Publishing Ltd on Apple Mac.
Printed and bound by CPI Group (UK) Ltd, Croydon, CR0 4YY.

Veloce Classic Reprint Series

Saab 96 & V4

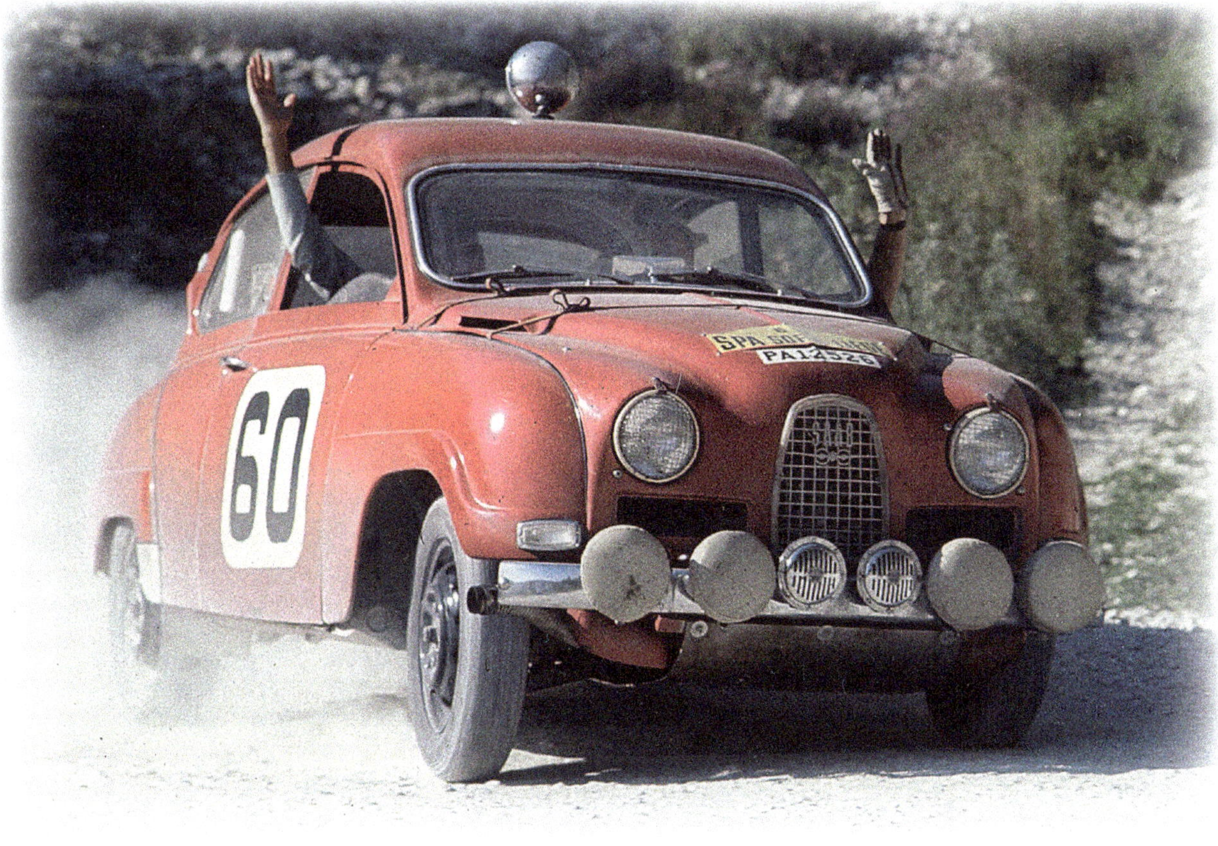

RALLY GIANTS

Graham Robson

Contents

Foreword .. 5
Introduction .. 7
Acknowledgements .. 8
The car and the team .. 9
    Inspiration .. 9
    The importance of the Saab 96 in rallying .. 11
    Facing up to rival cars .. 11
    Homologation – meeting the rules .. 12
    Engineering features .. 15
    93 – 'Father' of the 96 .. 18
    Enter the 96 .. 20
    V4 replaces straight three .. 27
    Motorsport development improvements .. 29
    Was the Saab 96 (and the V4) unique? .. 40
    Building and running the 'works' cars .. 41
    Personalities and star drivers .. 44
Competition story .. 55
    The 'works' Saab's career .. 55
    1960 .. 55
    1961 .. 59
    1962 .. 63
    1963 .. 67
    1964 .. 70
    1965 .. 80
    1966 .. 83
    1967 .. 86
    1968 .. 89
    1969 .. 94
    1970 .. 99
    1971 .. 101
    The long goodbye .. 105
    1972 .. 106
    1973 .. 108
    1974 .. 109
    1975 .. 110
    1976 .. 114
    Past its best? What rivals took over? .. 118
    How could Saab replace the V4? .. 119
World/major European rally wins .. 121
Index .. 127

Foreword

Rally Giants – the most important in the sport

What is a rally? Today's events, for sure, are completely different from those of a hundred, or even fifty years ago. What was once a test of reliability is now a test of speed and strength. What was once a long-distance trial is now a series of short-distance races.

In the beginning, rallying was all about using standard cars in long-distance road events, but by the 1950s the events were toughening up. Routes became rougher, target speeds were raised, point-to-point speed tests on special stages were introduced, and high-performance machines were needed to ensure victory.

Starting in the late 1950s teams started to develop extra-special versions of standard cars – built in small numbers and meant only for rallying or motor racing. These were the 'homologation specials' which now dominate the sport. The first of these, no question, was the Austin-Healey 3000, and the latest is any one of the ten-off World Rally Cars that we see on our TV screens, or on the special stages of the world.

Although rally regulations changed continuously over the years, two important developments stand out. The first was that four-wheel-drive was authorised from 1980. The second was that the 'World Rally Car' formula (which required only 20 identical cars to be produced to gain

homologation) was adopted in 1997. At all times, however, successful rally cars have needed to blend high performance with strength and reliability. Furthermore, and unlike Grand Prix cars, rally cars have needed to be built so that major repairs could be carried out at the side of the road, in the dark, sometimes in freezing cold, and sometimes in blazing temperatures.

Over the years, some cars became dominant, only to be eclipsed when new and more advanced rivals appeared. New cars appeared almost every year, but dramatically better machines appeared less often. From time to time, rally enthusiasts would be astonished by a new model, and it was on occasions like that when a new rallying landmark was set.

So, which were the most important new cars to appear in the last half century? What is it that made them special, at the time? In some cases it was perfectly obvious – Lancia's Stratos was the first ever purpose-built rally car, the Audi Quattro was the first rally-winning four-wheel-drive car, and the Toyota Celica GT4 was the first rally-winning four-wheel-drive Group A car to come from Japan.

But what about Saab's amazingly long-lived 96 and V4s? Or Ford's Escorts? Or the Fiat 131 Abarth? Or the Lancia Delta Integrale? Or, of course, the Subaru Impreza? All of them had something unique to offer at the time. Because they offered something different, and raised rallying's standards even further, they were true Rally Giants.

To a rallying petrol-head like me, it would have been easy to choose twenty, thirty or even more rally cars that have made a difference to the sport. However, I've had to be brutal, and cull my list to the very minimum. Listed here in chronological order, are the 'Rally Giants' I picked out to tell the on-going story of world-class rallying in the last fifty years:

Car	Period used as a 'works' car
Austin-Healey 3000	1959-1965
Saab 96 and V4	1960-1976
Mini-Cooper/Cooper S	1962-1970
Ford Escort Mk I	1968-1975
Lancia Stratos	1974-1981
Ford Escort Mk II	1975-1981
Fiat 131 Abarth	1976-1981
Audi Quattro and S1	1981-1986
Peugeot 205T16	1984-1986
Lancia Delta 4x4/Integrale	1987-1993
Toyota Celica GT4	1988-1995
Ford Escort RS Cosworth/WRC	1993-1998
Subaru Impreza Turbo/WRC	1993-2006

There is so much to know, to tell, and to enjoy about each of these cars that I plan to devote a compact book to each of them. And to make sure that one can be compared with another, I have kept to the same format for each volume.

Graham Robson

Introduction & Acknowledgements

Introduction

When the 1960s opened, all the headlines in European Championship rallies were increasingly dominated by two entirely different cars – the Austin-Healey 3000 and the Saab 96. The two could not have been more different. The Big Healey was all about brute power and high performance, whereas the Saab was an under-powered masterpiece that relied on an effective front-wheel-drive chassis, and superstar drivers.

Between 1960 and 1976, Saab achieved near miracles in rallying, for the 96 and its re-engined descendant, the 96 V4, were competitive throughout (but ... underpowered?). The two-stroke 96, with only 841cc, never had more than about 80bhp, while even the last and best of the V4s (bored to 1.8-litre) never had more than 175bhp at its disposal. All this, of course, was when the Swedish cars had to face 210bhp Austin-Healeys, 130bhp Lancia Fulvia HFs, and 250bhp Ford Escort RS1600s.

Without doubt, the Saab 96 and V4 family were Rally Giants. Any car that can boast World and European-level victories for so many years, in so many different locations, deserves that honour. Other cars – such as the Porsche 911 or the Alpine-Renault A110 – may have won as many events, but they never did so as modestly, so effectively, or so endearingly.

Although the Saab 96 was undoubtedly a great rally car, it's unlikely that the factory-backed machines would ever have gained such a reputation without the efforts of a handful of great drivers – and here I need only quote the names of Erik Carlsson, Carl-Magnus Skogh, Pat Moss, Simo Lampinen, Stig Blomqvist and Per Eklund, who all became supreme masters of this near-indestructible little Scandinavian machine.

If the Saab had a rallying secret, it was that (along with its remarkably dedicated drivers) it was a machine that never gave up. Sturdy in standard form, near bomb-proof when prepared to 'works' rally standards, and relatively simple to fettle and repair after the inevitable accident, it was a car that often got to the end of an event when a rival team might well have given up, and gone home in disgust.

Saab – the 'works' team, that is – always worked miracles with unpromising-looking machinery. How many other little departments could have extracted 175bhp from a very ordinary Ford-Germany V4 engine, when the Germans said that 105bhp was the absolute limit? How many other teams could expect an 80bhp two-stroke to be competitive against Supercars like the Mini-Cooper 1275S, yet beat them (in the right conditions) time after time?

'Works' Saabs had, of course, started rallying in the early 1950s, and the 3-cylinder 93 model had been winning since 1956. My story, however, begins with the 96, launched in 1960. Here was the definitive two-stroke car, where the front-wheel-drive, the flat-bottomed monocoque structure, and the useful transmission free-wheel all added up to a very effective little machine.

Even though funds were always limited, this was a range of cars that kept on improving, all the time attempting to keep abreast of its rivals. Disc front brakes arrived in 1962, the three-carburettor Saab Sport soon followed, a four-speed transmission soon found its way on to all models, and the much-torquier four-stroke 1.5-litre V4 followed in 1966. Progress, thereafter, was steady too – for there was an optional limited-slip differential from 1968, a 1.7-litre version of the engine from 1971, a twin-dual-choke Weber carburettor engine installation at about the same time, and a new cylinder head casting from 1973. Engines finally reached 1815cc (1933cc even, where homologation regulations did not apply), but the same basic four-speed transmission was used throughout.

With rare and honourable exceptions (a 95 estate car once, and a Saab Sonett Coupé on occasion), every 'works' car was a three cylinder Saloon, and, apart from regular changes to the front-end style, the shape and bulk of the machine never changed. One thing, of course, that never changed was the magnificent, supple, front-wheel-drive, which helped these outwardly ordinary cars to have the most remarkable roadholding and handling.

Although everyone – the team, the drivers, the opposition, and the media – realised that the 96 and V4 was regularly out-paced by its rivals, this never seemed to make the team down-hearted, or less than enthusiastic about their tasks. The cars were great, the drivers were brave, the team was likeable – and everyone enjoyed having them around.

A Rally Giant, then? No question ...

Acknowledgements

I couldn't possibly have completed this tribute to the front-wheel-drive Saabs without gaining a great deal of help from other experts and enthusiasts. Although I was already involved in International rallying when the Saab 96 was at its height, and knew many of the personalities involved, there was still much that I did not know about the cars themselves, and about the organisation that produced them.

Way back (yes, really, that far back) I got to know the principal characters in the team – Bosse Hellberg, Bo Swaner, Erik Carlsson and Gunnar Palm, in particular – and it was always a pleasure to talk rallying with them, and to pump them for information. Recently, it was a special pleasure for me to meet up once again with Bo Swaner, who rose to great things in the Saab organisation, and later became an influential administrator at World Rally Championship level.

Like many other rally enthusiasts of the time, I soon learned that if Erik Carlsson was rude to me (and he often was ...), then in a way he respected what I could do. On the other hand, by sitting alongside the Great Man, in a car, at media sessions, I realised that I could never even approach his expertise in driving a Saab.

Many other people, though, helped me over the years – not least Pat Moss, Stig Blomqvist and Per Eklund among the drivers, and several of the star mechanics too.

Even so, the most important character involved in providing many images, the rare-as-hen's teeth homologation papers, much archive information, and letting me look around some of the most famous cars, was Peter Backstrom, who manages the amazing Saab Car Museum in Trollhättan. When I started my research, and asked my contacts if they knew who might help me at Saab, the response was always: 'Ask Peter Backstrom – he knows everything ...'

So I did, and he does ... It would not have been possible without him.

Graham Robson

The car and the team

Inspiration

Let's be honest about this. Saab did not truly enter international rallying as part of a grand strategy to dominate the sport, but gradually found itself producing cars for events where new models like the twin-cylinder 92, and the three-cylinder 93 models might shine in their class, and in appropriate categories. It was not until the 1960s, when giants (in more ways than one) like Erik Carlsson and Carl-Magnus Skogh began to win events outright, that a more professional 'works' team evolved.

By the 1960s, for sure, when the cars covered in this book were closely involved, motorsport – rallying in particular – had got to the heart and soul of the company. The fact that the cars were winners in the right hands must

The famous badge, carried proudly on the nose of so many successful Saab 96s.

This was the original style and shape of the front-wheel-drive Saab, which was, of course, conceived by a company that had previously built aircraft. This was the original transverse-engined 92 of 1950.

Although Erik Carlsson won the RAC rally three times – 1960, 1961 and 1962 – he was not as lucky in 1959 with this 93B, when he crashed on a foggy night in Wales.

have helped, but in any case the giant-killing antics of the team drivers – Erik Carlsson and (later) Stig Blomqvist in particular – must have helped. Sweden, geographically large, but remote from the wider world in many ways, needed to show off its excellence. Saab, just one part of Sweden, took the same view, and was justly proud of the way its rallying exploits built a strong image.

It is fair, I think, to suggest that if Saabs had not been built in Scandinavia, where the company expanded strongly during the 1950s, the same period that Scandinavian rallies had embraced loose-surfaced special stage motoring, then the marque's reputation in rallying might have been limited. In mainland Europe, it was all very well seeing heroines like Greta Molander winning Ladies' awards, but there was no way that an underpowered Saab (even in 1958, the 750GT version of the 93 produced only 45bhp) could win on Tarmac rallies where speed hill-climbs and circuit races were so prominent.

The true inspiration, however, came after 1956, when the three-cylinder Saab 93 took over from the original twin-cylinder 92. Although the engine was still not large, or over-endowed with spare power, it was at least more likely to take on real competition from other European makes. Not only that, it was also in 1956 that the first outright rally victories were achieved, and as year followed year, individual performances turned into great team efforts.

The final impetus, which made the front-wheel-drive Saab even more competitive, came in 1960, when the 748cc Model 93 was replaced by the 841cc Model 96. From this moment on (if only for two years or so) the Saab was at least the equal of other front-wheel-drive cars like the little BMC Mini (which had 848cc), and the DKWs of the period – and in drivers like Carl-Magnus Skogh and Erik Carlsson it also had the best and bravest loose-surfaced rally-driving heroes in the world.

The importance of the Saab 96 in rallying

Here we must look inwards and become more parochial. By world standards the Saab 96 was never vitally important, if only because it was not fast enough, and not suited to events on tarmac, or on events where speed and acceleration uphill was critical to achieving a good result. It was, on the other hand, superb on loose surface going, on ice and snow, and anywhere where rugged strength and front-wheel-drive traction was desirable.

Above all else, it emphasised that front-wheel-drive cars could be competitive in certain types of rallying. Up until that time, most competitive cars had featured front-engine/rear-wheel-drive layouts, and were invariably expensive machines. It was not until the first Porsches came on the scene that the advantage of having an engine-over-driving-wheels layout became apparent. Then, in certain circumstances, the advantage of engine-over-wheels and steering those wheels added to the package ...

It was for all these reasons that the 96 was an important car in Scandinavia, but less so in the wider world. When Saab started preparing very lightly-modified 92s and 93s in the 1950s, it either had to be content with Ladies' Awards (Greta Molander won a whole raft of such prizes), or began to figure on Scandinavian events, where snow and ice (winter) or gravel (summer) special stages were always used. Saab, for sure, enjoyed winning at home, especially if it could humiliate Volvo (the big Swedish rival) or VW (who had a big market share), but saw little point in spending money on summer events on the Mediterranean, or in markets where its cars were not strongly marketed.

Somehow, though, the cars were not 'sexy' – and private owners could usually find an excuse to buy another, more fashionable, machine. Even though Erik Carlsson set a series of magnificent records, why should a privateer buy a Saab when he could buy a Mini-Cooper, which was much cheaper? As far as Saab was concerned, however, the importance of rallying to the 96 was that it emphasised the reliability and strength of the car's design – and it was almost

Front-wheel-drive

Although Saab was the first Swedish car maker to use front-wheel-drive, the company was not a pioneer of that technology in Europe. Way back in 1931, DKW of Germany (itself already a well-respected motorcycle manufacturer) introduced a new 'peoples' car, one which not only had front-wheel-drive, but also used a compact two-cylinder two-stroke engine which it had already been using for three years. During the 1930s, and on into the war years (in which Sweden remained steadfastly neutral) Saab made a study of many of Europe's economy cars, and it was no coincidence that it eventually chose a layout very similar to that of the DKW Reichsklasse and Meisterklasse models. Although there was no question of common components being used, an experienced engineer could certainly study the original Saab, and see that some aspects of DKW technology had impressed Saab's designers.

incidental that it also confirmed the unearthly loose-surface driving skills of heroes like Erik Carlsson and Carl-Magnus Skogh.

Facing up to rival cars

This was the competition with which the Saab 96 and later the Saab V4, was faced on the International rally scene in the 1960s and 1970s. Many of these cars were limited-production, rather specialised, 'homologation specials,' which made it difficult for Saab, which was a much more 'production-based' rally car, to compete:

Mini-Cooper and Mini-Cooper S – transversely-mounted front engine/front-wheel-drive. Cooper first used in 1962, 1071S in 1963, and the definitive 1275S from 1964 to 1968. In terms of handling and balance, always the equal of the Saab, with a fleet of superstar drivers to match Erik Carlsson, Stig Blomqvist and their kin. Much lighter that any other rally car of the period, with a better power/weight ratio. Structurally and technically fragile at first, but once made reliable, and with up to 110-120bhp from 1275cc, they set many standards. Three Monte Carlo victories and a European Championship tell their own story. Like the Saab, eventually overwhelmed by Alpine-Renault, Porsche and Ford.

Volvo PV544 and 120 'Amazon' series – front-engine/rear-drive. Too conventional, and not specialised enough to become consistent winners, but with drivers like Gunnar Andersson and Tom Trana could be superb on rough endurance events. After Karl-Magnus Skogh moved over from Saab to Volvo for 1963, the team was even stronger than before. Strong if not ultra-powerful, Volvos could win on demanding events (like the Acropolis and Safari), were often competitive in their native Scandinavia, but usually outpaced in Europe, especially where tarmac special stages figured in the routes. No longer competitive after c.1965.

Ford Cortina GT and Lotus-Cortina – front engine/rear-drive. GT used regularly from 1963, Lotus-Cortina regularly used from 1965. Backed by large budgets, and Ford's determination to become a 'world' rallying power. Light but well-balanced (though structurally fragile at first), gradually developed, strengthened and made more reliable with the passing years. Lacking in traction on loose and icy/snow surfaces, but with a large operating budget, superstar drivers, and Ford's great determination to win. Soon succeeded by:

Ford Escort Twin-Cam, RS1600 and RS1800 – front-engine/rear-drive. Arrived in 1968, when the Mini-Cooper S was at its peak, and soon came to establish dominance. Originally with Lotus-Cortina running gear, then with dedicated Cosworth 16-valve engines, persistently faster and more durable than many rivals. Also lacking in traction on loose surfaces/ice/snow, but backed by Ford's great determination. The Escort would go on to have a 13-year career at the top. Even at the end, it was still capable of winning 'world' rallies, and entire Championships.

Porsche 911 – rear-engine/rear-drive. A carefully-engineered sports coupé, first used in 1965. Already available in a 160bhp/2.0-litre version at that time with much more to come. Superb traction. Vic Elford would win the European Championship, in 1967, and the Monte Carlo rally in 1968: Bjorn Waldegård would then win two Montes in larger-engined cars. There was always much more potential in this car than Porsche ever employed, though it was gradually realised in later years. Rivals were relieved that Porsche chose to concentrate on circuit racing.

Alpine-Renault A110 – rear engine/rear-drive. First used in 1964. Tubular back-bone chassis frame, and ultra-light GRP body shell. Available with 1.3-litre engine from 1965, with more to come – after the Mini years it would be enlarged to 1.8-litres. Superb traction. Still fragile in the mid-1960s, not yet a winner, but sure to be so when reliability was gained. World Championships and Monte Carlo rally victories were all achieved in the 1970s. Budgets expanded to match ambitions – which resulted in Makes Championship wins in 1971 and 1973.

Lancia Fulvia HF – front-engine, front-drive. First used in 1966. A 1.2-litre, then 1.3-litre, at this time, but with 1.6-litre/5-speed transmission set to come in 1968/1969 – and superb traction. Not always powerful enough to win everywhere, but over the years a seemingly enormous budget made up for much of that. Lancia, it seemed, would always pay handsomely for success, but came to expect it of all its drivers, engineers and team members.

Homologation – meeting the rules

Here was a case – a rare case, I have to say, in modern rallying – where no artifice was ever practised, or needed, to get a particular model approved for use in motorsport. Although Saab always seemed to be a transparently honest company, and had no overt ambition to be 'best-at-any-price,' the fact that its rally cars were always closely related to its series production machines became an increasing problem for the team.

The newly-launched Saab Sport of 1963 was a well-equipped little car, even more suitable for rallying than the original 96 had been.

When the Saab 96 was first announced, the only existing example of what became known as a rallying 'homologation special' was the Austin-Healey 3000, the specification of which was still developing. By comparison with the Saab 96, this ferocious car was twice as powerful (but considerably

The Monster! Would it have made a good competition car? Early in the 1960s, and just for fun, Saab built up this 1.7-litre, six-cylinder, two-stroke prototype – three cylinders at each side of the front-wheel-drive transmission – but found that it was very nose-heavy and suffered severe handling problems. A good idea at the time, though …

heavier), and could be expected to set fastest times wherever its driven rear wheels could get grip.

As explained further in the next section, the original 'works' car to be homologated was the basic Saab 96, that homologation becoming valid from March 1960. This car had only just gone on sale in the first weeks of 1960, and more than 20,000 were produced in that year alone. This meant that Group 1 homologation (5000 cars to be built) was easily achieved, and in fact the actual rate of production achieved surged ahead in future years.

The next big performance upgrade came with the 96 Sport, an additional model with a 52bhp/841cc engine, which was launched in February 1962, and homologated in May 1963. Although this sounds like (and was) a very creditable power increase, we should remember that the BMC Mini-Cooper (55bhp, 997cc, smaller and just as nimble as the Saab) had already gone on sale, and that the 70bhp/1071cc Mini-Cooper S would follow it in 1963. Because of Saab's limited size, and available finance, this was as close to an homologation special version of the 96 as the little Swedish company ever made.

Finally, the Ford V4-engined Saab 96 V4 took over in the summer of 1966, was homologated without any artifice in the next few months (the official date listed in FIA No. 5125 was 1 November 1966), and would become the team's rally car of choice from 1967 onwards: the first 'works' use was in the Swedish rally of February 1967. In one form or another (and by taking every legitimate advantage of allowances and provisions in the FIA's Appendix J), it was the V4 that was used as the company's front line rally car for the next ten years.

No sooner had the V4 engine been adopted than Saab (not Ford-Germany, who really had no motorsport interest in its own V4, as opposed to the V6 to which it was closely related) began to look for ways to power tune it. Ford-Germany put much effort into power-tuning the V6 – using it, for instance, in the Capri RS2600s which won the European Touring car Championship in 1971 and 1972, but never applied that knowledge to the V4. Originally, Ford-Germany told Saab that no more than 105bhp was ever going to be possible from the 1.5-litre V4; even so, by 1968, twin-carburettor 'Group 5' or 'Group 6' prototype engines with up to 140bhp were already running, and further improvements would be made.

The last, and very significant, change came in 1970, for this was the year in which US-specification V4 production cars began to be fitted with the 1698cc V4 engine. Not only was this engine speedily homologated for rally and other motorsport purposes, but because the car was now running in the 1.5-2.0-litre class, that engine itself could be enlarged even further. 'Works' cars ran with 1740cc or even 1815cc derivatives, and were habitually fitted with two sidedraught twin-choke Weber carburettors, these being built on 'cross-over' manifolds with lengthy inlet tracts, so that the Weber feeding the two cylinders on one side of the car were actually placed on the other side of the engine bay. 155bhp was normal in this condition, and that peak power output would be pushed up further during the 1970s – the very last engines were rated at approximately 175bhp.

Towards the end of the V4's life, Saab persuaded Ford-Germany to push the casting technology and the layout of the V4 engine to the absolute limit, and occasionally used 1933cc engines (in events where the regulations allowed it), which were not only at the absolute limit as far as cylinder bore dimensions were concerned, but which gave the four-speed manual transmission a very hard time.

As the V4 engines gradually became more and more powerful, the limits of this transmission were always the Achilles heel of the V4's layout, for the search for further alternatives was always constrained by the front-wheel-drive layout. As Ford, Fiat, and (later) Vauxhall all demonstrated, it was always possible, and 'sporting-legal' to have complete alternative gearboxes, and alternative final drive assemblies to be homologated, but these were relatively simple front-engine/rear-drive cars, built up on what we might rather unkindly call the 'Lego' principle. This was not possible for the Saab 96, where the gearbox casing was integral with that covering the final drive, and where the two mechanisms were closely linked.

Svenska Aeroplan AB – the parent company

It was as recently as 1937 that a company called Svenska Aeroplan Aktiebolaget was set up at Trollhättan – about 35 miles/55 kilometres north of Gothenburg – where the existing strategy was to produce military aircraft. Although the Swedish government had no intention of getting involved in the Second World War (an outbreak, even in 1937, seemed to be an imminent possibility), it was determined to build up the Swedish Air Force to be able to defend itself if attacked.

Although the obvious acronym of this company was SAAB, it was not long before the more conventional 'Saab' was adopted for the company and its products. Original products included licence-built Junkers (bomber) and Grumman (fighter) aircraft, but the company's first own-design fighter, the B17, followed in 1940, and a small civil airliner, the Saab 90 Scandia, first flew in 1946.

The only way for Saab to follow suit on its front-wheel-drive car would have been to design, develop, build and put into production a completely new gearbox/final drive/transaxle system. The cost of doing this was such that a relatively modestly-financed team like Saab could not readily tackle it. Furthermore, not only would a thousand such assemblies have had to be specially made (and counted, for approval, by FIA inspectors), and put on sale, but they would have had to be priced at a level which might not have appealed to many Saab private owners. Life can be unfair to an underdog sometimes ...

As with other manufacturers, Saab also took advantage of a concession allowing it to homologate lightweight items. From 1 January 1970, lightweight steel doors, along with 'Plexiglass' side and rear windows were approved. The last significant motorsport change, which helped the V4 engine to produce a very creditable power output, was the development of a much-modified cylinder head design, which featured twin exhaust ports per head (the mass-produced heads had just one siamesed port). This was homologated on 1 July 1973.

Saab, to its great credit, tried to keep abreast of developments in the sport as much as possible, publishing commendably detailed lists of motorsport parts, and making them available to private owners. Although the design of the front-wheel-drive Saab V4 was effectively rendered obsolete by specialised machines such as the Alpine-Renault A110, and the Lancia Stratos, the last outright victory at world level would come in 1976 – no less than sixteen years after the first – which gave the 96-based car a remarkably long career.

Engineering features

Until dedicated 'homologation specials' such as the BMC Mini-Cooper S, and the Ford Escort Twin-Cam, came along, the Saab 96 seemed to have the ideal basic layout for a rally car. With front-wheel-drive, a rock-solid unit-construction shell, and very simply-engineered running gear, there was much to encourage its use in world-class, rough-and-tough motorsport.

Originally, the Saab's basic layout dated from 1945-1947 – when the modest Swedish company, which had previously made its living building military (mostly) and civil (a few) aircraft, decided to diversify. Management, it seemed, concluded that there was an opening, a demand even, in Sweden for a new type of family car. The only Swedish car company in existence at that time was Volvo (making medium-size and larger models), so Saab elected to develop a smaller car instead.

But what sort of car? Market analysis showed that in recent years, in the 1930s, the German DKW had been the best-selling small car in Sweden, so it seems reasonable that Saab should study that car's layout closely when developing its own new model – to be called the Saab 92.

This Saab archive shot shows how the basic style altered gradually from the 1950s to the 1970s. Left-to-right: 1950 Saab 92, 1956 Saab 93, 1960 Saab 96, 1966 V4, and the last V4 of all built in 1980.

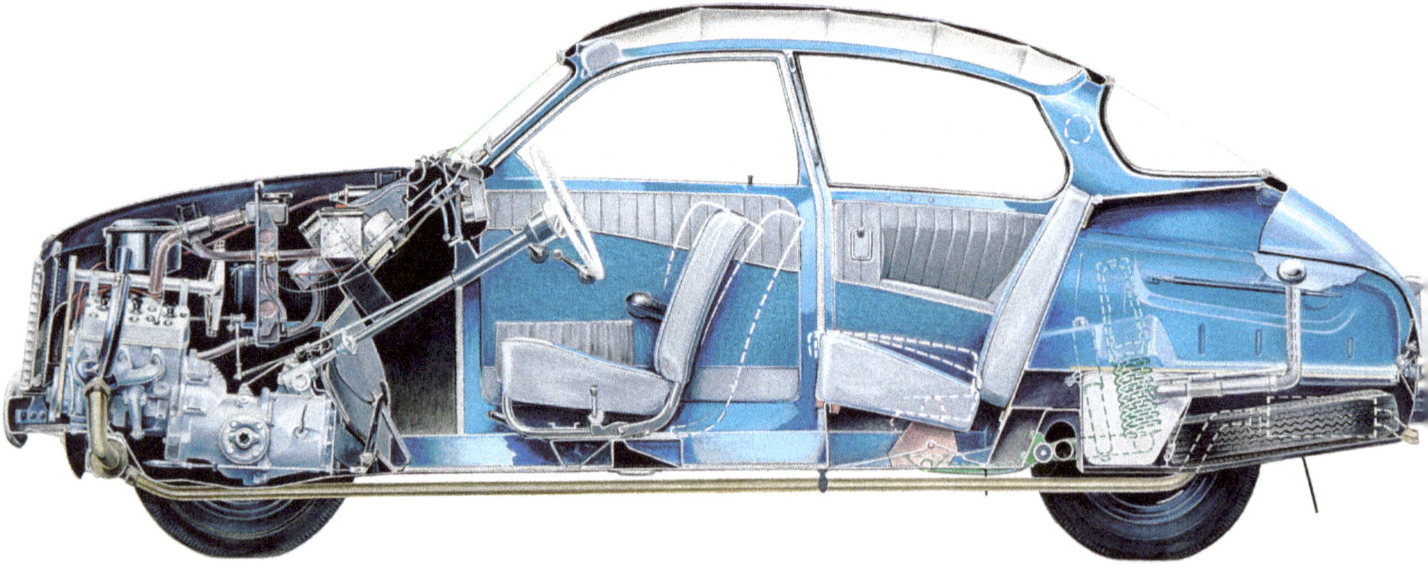

This stunningly-detailed 'ghosted' cross-section of a 96 shows just how compact the engine bay of the car actually was, and also emphasises the flat floor of the unit-construction body shell.

Because Sweden remained resolutely neutral during the Second World War, there was a little time to sit back and ponder the company's future. Accordingly, the original Saab production car, which went on sale at the end of 1949, had some features that were clearly inspired by DKW, though there was no question of what I might call 'Japanese-copy' methods being carried out.

The style of the original car, influenced, no question, by the company's ever-growing experience of aviation aerodynamics, was a two-door fastback Saloon, with no external access to the luggage boot. (Other cars of the period, notably the original (British) Standard Eight of 1953, suffered from the same drawback). The Saab style was curved, positively ovoid, in all directions, with the headlamps recessed, and air entering the engine bay through a wide but shallow front grille. No doubt it is a cynical comment, but it was amazing that early rally drivers found that the shape of the Saab, which had no sharp corners, allowed cars to be easily righted after they had inadvertently been rolled ...

Because the original car featured a transversely-mounted, two-cylinder two-stroke engine, integral transmission, and front-wheel-drive, the engine bay was very compact, and this meant that no important mechanical bulk protruded into the passenger compartment, for there was no propeller shaft making its way to the rear. This meant that from the toe-board backwards, the floor of the unit-construction shell could effectively be almost flat, and the rear suspension could also be made simple, as no allowance for a differential or driveshafts had to be made.

Few people actively involved in motorsport thought much about this car at the time, as its 25bhp/764cc engine guaranteed no more than 62-65mph, with leisurely acceleration from its three-speed gearbox (which had synchromesh on top and second gears and a freewheel), so they probably did not notice how ideal the body shell would be for use on loose-surfaced rallies or over snow and ice, where a shield under the front-end was all that was needed to turn this machine into a four-seater 'toboggan.' It was not for years that the advantage of having a freewheel – that one could, if necessary, change gear without using the clutch pedal – became apparent in rallying. The suspension, too, was supple, and suited to driving along the loose surfaces with which the whole of Scandinavia abounded. At this stage, by the way, front and rear suspension were independent, by transverse torsion bars – expensive, but effective.

Once production cars began to be seen all over Sweden, and in several export countries, the basic design was soon accepted. Although two-stroke engines were already regarded as rather old-fashioned, and limited machines, the 92 seemed to work very well, so Saab's big financial gamble in entering the automotive market seemed to be justified.

Caution, rather than reckless flair, however, was always the policy at Trollhättan, so for the next twenty-five years, Saab spent more time on refining the existing basic design, rather than searching for a new layout, and it was this gradual improvement of the basic 92 layout which eventually led to the sturdy, if still under-powered 96 of 1960. Since most significant changes were carried forward to future models, it is clear that improvements to the 93, to the original Sonett sports car, and in particular the 750GT of the late 1950s would all benefit the 96, when it arrived.

Even at an early stage, Saab realised that the use of a two-cylinder two-stroke engine, and a three-speed transmission, would eventually limit the performance of the road cars, and perhaps restrict their appeal. However, a limited motorsport programme, in which Saab engineer Rolf Melde became prominent, helped to keep the cars in the credible forefront of the 'small car' market.

From the end of 1952, therefore, the original 92 gave way to the 92B, the basic difference being that external access to the luggage 'boot' was finally available, and at the same time a much larger rear window was provided. By 1954 the engine output had been raised to 28bhp, which might have been competitive on the road cars, but did little for rally car performance.

Saab, meanwhile, was developing its own-design three-cylinder two-stroke engine, which was first seen on the very limited-production Saab Sonett Super Sport two-seater. Its main marketing thrust, however, was to power the Saab

93, which was introduced at the very end of 1955. This car was considerably different in many ways from the 92B, the true direct ancestor of the 96, and therefore of all the rally cars described in this book. Not only did it have a new engine, but also a new transmission, new suspension all round, and new style.

93 – 'Father' of the 96

Except for the nose, which was nearly four inches longer to accommodate the new engine and its associated radiator (described below), and featured a new vertical grille of a type which all such Saab Saloons and estates would carry for a decade, the structure of the 93 was based on that of the 92B. Under the skin, though, all was new.

The truly major innovation was that now there was a new three-cylinder, two-stroke engine, which was mounted in-line (rather than transverse, as with the 92 and 92B), and inclined at 30 degrees towards the left side of the engine bay, which was allied to a new design of front-wheel-drive transaxle, with three forward gears (and, if we had known it at the time, provision for a four-speed transmission within a modified case). Although DKW of Germany had recently announced a similar engine, and a Germany-based consultant, an ex-DKW engineer, had also worked on Saab's new power unit, there was no link between the two, and no common parts.

The new engine, in other words, might have had more moving parts – seven instead of five, which is to say three pistons, three connecting rods and one crankshaft – but actually had a slightly smaller swept volume, but significantly more peak power and torque. This power unit was allied to a new transmission unit, where the main gearbox was mounted behind the line of the final drive.

It was time, it seemed, for some costs to be taken out of the chassis, as the original torsion bar suspension of the

Saab rally cars came a long way in a short time. This is a mid-1950s 93, an under-powered, but usually bravely-driven machine.

Model	Engine type	Bore x stroke (mm)	Capacity (cc)	Peak power (bhp/rpm)
92/92B	2-cylinder, 2-stroke Transverse-mounted	80x76	764	25-28/3800
93	3-cylinder, 2-stroke In-line mounted	66x73	748	33/4200

How the new and old Saab engines compared.

Engines don't come much simpler than this. When the Saab 93 was introduced in the 1950s it featured a three-cylinder, two-stroke engine, with just seven moving parts – three pistons, three connecting rods, and one crankshaft. In 'works' 96 rally form the 841cc engine eventually produced up to 80bhp.

Rallying, pre-96 style, on the GP circuit at Zandvoort in Holland. This was the final test in the Tulip Rally of 1958, with 93Bs at the head of a field that also included Austin A35s, Renault Dauphines and Morris Minor 1000s.

92 and 92B had been dumped, in favour of coil springs and wishbones at the front, along with coil springs and telescopic dampers controlling a 'dead' beam axle at the rear. By this time, annual Saab production was already approaching 10,000 cars a year, which meant that there was never likely to be a problem in homologating a car for motorsport, where 1000 cars/year (Group 2) or 5000/year (Group 1 – 'showroom standard') were required.

Between 1956 and 1960, however, further innovations all led inexorably towards the definitive 96. First of all, in 1958, came the GT750 Saloon, which was a car particularly intended for sale in the USA, having a 45bhp version of the modern three-cylinder engine, along with a much higher level of interior equipment. This car was the forerunner of what would become the Saab 96 Sport/Monte Carlo, and therefore had an important place in the family tree.

Next, in 1959, the Saab 95 Estate car was introduced, a car that had no obvious application in motorsport (though, to suit the regulations of that event, Erik Carlsson would drive one in the 1961 Monte Carlo rally), but once again one which had an important bearing on what would come in the 96 Saloon. First of all, it was the first Saab to be fitted with the definitive 841cc three-cylinder engine and, to help maintain the performance of what was a heavier car than the existing 93 Saloon, it was fitted with a four-speed gearbox, still controlled by a steering column change.

Enter the 96

No sooner had the 95 Estate been introduced than the 96 Saloon also appeared. First seen in February 1960, when revealed to the media at a launch in Stockholm, it went on general sale in March 1960, when it took over completely from the popular 93 series. Once again, this was evolutionary rather than revolutionary, for the style was much as before, the chassis was almost exactly as before, with the large changes coming to the engine, and to the rear end of the body.

As in the 95 Estate car, the engine was to be a 38bhp/841cc two-stroke power unit, though in the new Saloon the three-speed transmission would be retained for the time being. The style/rear-end structure of the body shell showed a more capacious shape over the rear seats, much larger rear quarter windows, and a wrap-around rear window which Saab claimed to be 117 per cent larger than before. The boot compartment was larger, and was fitted with a redesigned lid. Not only that, but now it also hid a 40-litre fuel tank. Here at last was the definitive front-wheel-drive/two-stroke-engined Saab body shape, structure and general style, which was to become so very familiar in motorsport in future years.

Yet there were many more changes to come, most of which were of great benefit to the competition cars. The four-speed box which became a feature of the load-carrying 95 Estate car at the time, was added to the specification of the 96 Saloon from late 1961, but only for certain countries (it was not, for instance, available in the UK). The next big step forward therefore came in February 1962, with the launch of the Saab 96 Sport (it was known as Granturismo 850 in the USA ...), which not only included a triple-Solex carburettor installation for the three-cylinder engine, but a nominal compression ratio of 9.0:1, and a peak power output of 52bhp. The lubrication system was updated, to a 'total-loss' pump supply system via external piping, so that it was no longer necessary to use the archaic method of mixing oil with petrol when refuelling the car. Not only this, but the four-speed gearbox (with freewheel) was standardised, and front-wheel disc brakes by Lockheed were fitted.

In many ways, this update was almost as important as that carried out by BMC when updating the Mini 850 into the Mini-Cooper just a few months earlier. This, then, was the car used by the rally team until 1967 when the V4 came along. From 1963/1964, incidentally, the 850 Sport officially became the 96 Monte Carlo (this was to commemorate Erik Carlsson's fine double victories of 1962 and 1963), though there were few important technical changes to flag up that change.

Because of the major boost in power output, the 96 Sport's performance was, of course, considerably better

Except in decorative detail, the rear-end style of the 96 and V4 models did not change from 1960 to 1977.

The Saab 96 was little known in the wider world until the rally successes began to accumulate. This was the original-shape car of the early 1960s.

Although the 96 Saloon was always the more glamorous of this family of Saabs, the 95 Estate cars were extremely useful, and practical, load carriers.

This excellent cutaway study shows the very compact front-wheel-drive layout of the original Saab 96. The engine was placed well ahead of the line of the front wheels, there was a roomy four-seater cabin, and the rear suspension was a simple 'dead' axle.

This was the Saab Sport engine of the early 1960s, where the triple-choke carburettor looked to be almost as large as the cylinder block itself!

Although the Saab 96 engine was a small 841cc unit, there was precious little space in the engine bay to install it. Amazingly, the 1.5-litre 60-degree V4 unit that followed would fit into the same space!

Even in the early 1970s, the front suspension of the works-prepared V4 looked little different from standard.

The Saab Sport two-stroke engine featured a big triple-choke carburettor, and was mated to a four-speed gearbox.

For styling and marketing reasons, Saab made several changes to the shape of the front end, which originally had round headlamps, and later rectangular headlamps. Rally cars were seen with all the different front ends, for the homologation papers took account of the changes.

Erik Carlsson (left) and Bo Hellberg assessing the Sonett Sports Coupé, to see if it had any sporting potential. Unhappily, unless the handicap applied to a particular event was in its favour, the Saloon was usually a better bet.

Two-stroke engines

At the time the original Saab 92 was designed, in the 1940s, the two-stroke engine was the cheapest and simplest known way of turning petrol into power. Because there were no inlet or exhaust valves, or valve gear, such engines were very simple and cheap to manufacture, though mechanically inefficient. Saab and others, for instance, made much of the fact that there were only seven moving parts in a three-cylinder, two-stroke engine – three pistons, three connecting rods, and one crankshaft.

The entire combustion cycle was completed in just one engine revolution. Fuel-air mixture was drawn in to the cylinder/crankcase, then compressed by the piston as it descended into that crankcase. The compressed gas then transferred to the top end of the engine by ports cut into the cylinder wall, and when the piston returned to the top of its stroke, combustion took place. As the piston then descended on the 'power' stroke, the exit gas was expelled through another port in the cylinder wall: in the meantime, the under-side of the piston was already compressing the next charge of fuel-air ...

Invention of the two-stroke cycle is attributed to Sir Dugald Clerk in 1878, who shortly patented it, and in due course engines using it proved to be very popular in many small-power-unit applications, and in motorcycles. The first two-stroke engined production cars were sold by DKW of Germany in 1928 and sold well all over Europe, the engines being studied carefully by Saab before the Swedish concern launched its own products.

Two-strokes had important advantages and drawbacks. Advantages included the cheapness of manufacture, compact size, and ease of servicing. Unfortunately, the two-stroke process was thermodynamically not very efficient – although 'works' Saab rally cars eventually had up to 80/85bhp from their 841cc engines, this was achieved with one power stroke per revolution – which compared badly with, say, a similar output from a four-stroke engine with only one power stroke for every other revolution.

Crankshaft lubrication usually relied on the mixing of oil with petrol (in the fuel tank) when it was first pumped into the car. Later Saab 96s (including the Sport/Monte Carlo models) had a separate oil feed process, but this was still a 'total loss' installation, which was costly in its use of oil, and levels needed constant vigilance on the part of the driver. All two-stroke cars tended to leave behind them a blue haze of exhaust smoke, which even in the 1960s offended many environmentalists.

than that of the basic 96. *Autocar's* road test, published in February 1965, flagged up a top speed of 88mph, 0-60mph in 19.1sec, and a standing-quarter mile sprint in 21.2sec. Overall fuel consumption, at 20.7mpg, was poor – but Saab enthusiasts didn't mind that. This, of course, reflected the way that from mid-1962 (when the Sport was homologated) the 'works' rally cars were significantly faster than before.

In the next few years, however, the only significant upgrade came in 1964, when the front-end style of the entire 95/96 range of cars was changed, without affecting the overall bulk of the machine. Henceforth, the main radiator grille would be much deeper, but slimmer, and it was flanked by large air intakes on each side: all-in-all, the 96 was just six inches/150mm longer than before. Whereas the original 96 had featured an entire front-end/bonnet that could be lifted in one movement, the latest car featured a fixed grille/nose, and there was a more conventional bonnet panel. All the original long-bonnet cars had circular headlamps, but rectangular lamps would take over from the start of the 1969 model year.

The visual effect was pleasing, and the engineering effect was to allow a lot more cooling air get into the engine bay, which was a boost, as the power output of the Sport had been raised to 55bhp. Soon after this the 'Sport' became the 'Monte Carlo' in some territories, but the two cars were really one and the same. Once introduced, incidentally, there would be no further changes of any nature to the existing chassis while the 96 and V4 range was still in production – a period that would stretch until the end of the 1970s.

V4 replaces straight three

The next major change came in September 1966 when (advertised as an 'additional model,' but that was only a marketing ruse to help clear stocks of the old two-stroke cars) the four-stroke-engined Saab V4 took over from the Saab 96. Internally, incidentally, the V4 was the 'Saab 98,' but this notation was never used in public. As noted in the panel on page 34 the engine was the very compact 1498cc V4 power unit (with a 60-degree vee angle, which had a counter-rotating balancer shaft to improve the engine in terms of vibration and balance) manufactured in Cologne by Ford-Germany, and already used in many of its existing private cars and light commercial vehicles. It was not at all related to the Ford-of-Britain V4s that had recently gone on sale, and which were found in products as diverse as the Ford Zephyr 4 and the Transit van!

Because the German V4 was such a compact power unit (it was at least as wide as it was long), it fitted easily into the existing style and structure. In many ways (and this typified Saab's budget-conscious approach to business) this 65bhp car was a rather simple 'minimum-change' machine, for there had been no change to the style, the structure, or to the rest of the running gear of the car, which in turn had been minor evolutions of those of the previous Saab 96 Sport model. All of this meant that the four-speed transmission, the front-wheel disc brakes and the suspension would all be familiar to technicians and dealerships all around the world. At the time, Saab made the point that the new car's performance should be on a par with a 998cc Mini-Cooper – but, then, so it should be, as the V4 was a 1.5-litre car.

Even before the rally team got its hands on the car, personalities pointed out that well over 100bhp would

The V4-engined car took over from the two-stroke 96 in the summer of 1966. V4-engined cars then remained in production until 1980.

be available in Group 2 form, which would give a real performance boost to the rally car in future seasons. The statistics, however, did not tell the whole story, for in rally form the V4 had much more mid-range torque than the two-stroke type had ever enjoyed. Indeed, the razor-edge tune two-strokes had very creditable peak torque and power figures, but were apt to misfire at anything below mid-range, and would not pull strongly until something close to peak revs was achieved.

V4 engine sizes – 'works' rally cars

Within the same basic cylinder block, and always within the same cylinder bore centre locations, several different engine sizes were used by the 'works' cars between 1966 and 1976. The most significant were as follows:

Capacity (cc)	Bore and stroke (mm)	Comment
1498	90 x 58.9	As originally homologated in 1966
1698	90 x 66.8	As homologated from 1971
1740	91 x 66.8	Enlarged from 1698cc by an over-bore
1815	93 x 66.8	Further enlargement, bored to the limit on selected blocks
1933	96 x 66.8	Final enlargement of very large bore, only available with re-cored (and therefore non-homologated) cylinder blocks.

The road car, indeed, was considerably faster than both its predecessors – 96 and 96 Sport – had ever been. *Autocar* tried a car in 1967, noting that it had a top speed of 92mph (20mph faster than that of the original Saab 96, of course) with 0-60mph in 16.5 seconds, and a standing quarter-mile dash in 20.0sec. Although the V4 was perhaps 50kg/110lb heavier than the old 96 had been, it was at least 50 per cent more powerful, and the trade-off was certainly worthwhile.

All this, and the retention of a freewheel, made the new car not only more desirable as a road car proposition, but showed off the potential of the competition cars. As far as motorsport was concerned, it all looked very promising. The story goes that Erik Carlsson and Bo Swaner shared a car at the Press launch, and during the drive Erik turned to Bo and quipped: "Hey, I like this one so much that I can now start recommending it to my friends as well ..."

In the next few years, Saab made a series of changes to the V4, though these were all in detail, and not in layout or philosophy. One reason for this was that management, and the engineering team, were increasingly tied up with finalising the new Saab range, the 99, which not only had an entirely different structure, but was to use a new overhead-camshaft four-stroke engine to be manufactured by Triumph in the UK.

For 1968, the windscreen and the rear window were increased in size, and there was a serious revision to the fascia layout. Then, for 1969, the front-end/grille was revised, notably with the addition of rectangular headlamps on all but USA-market models. Just before the end of the decade, Saab (in conjunction with OY Valmet AB) opened a new car assembly plant at Uusikaupunki in Finland. In future years this would allow Saab to enter rallies for its Finnish stars driving nominally Finnish-built V4s.

Although the new-generation 99 took most of the headlines as the 1970s opened, V4 sales held up remarkably well. In 1970, no fewer than 34,120 such Saloons and 9367 Estate cars were built. 1970 models got recessed fuel filler caps, 1971 models got headlamp wiper/washer fittings as standard (not in the USA) – but because of the sporting connotations, for 1971 the USA-market cars got 65bhp/1.7-litre V4 engines.

As far as the production cars were concerned, the larger

engine, lightly tuned, was necessary for Saab to meet the latest exhaust emissions regulations in the USA, but for the rally team it meant it could use an 11 per cent larger engine, which ought to deliver at least that extra amount of torque.

Although the V4 still had an enthusiastic clientele, sales in the 1970s then gradually ebbed away – 22,762 Saloons and 5559 Estate cars were sold in 1974. Amazingly, however, few important mechanical changes were made to the cars during the 1970s. The last V4 estate car was built in 1978, while the very last V4 Saloon was produced on 7 January 1980. This was thought to be such an important, and such a nostalgic occasion, that Erik Carlsson was asked to drive it off the line at the Finnish plant – after which it was immediately delivered to the Saab museum in Trollhättan, where it became a prime exhibit.

Motorsport development and improvements

Right from the start, Saab realised that it would always be seen as an underdog, because it used a small engine of old and (some said) obsolete design. That was one drawback. Another was that there was officially no separate, dedicated

This shot shows the flat underside of the Saab 96 and V4, which made it ideal for passing over loose and rough surfaces without sustaining much damage. The picture dates from 1969.

A quaint little detail vignette – BP sponsored Saab's rally team in the 1960s. Before the separate-oil-supply-engine was developed, BP supplied this special 'two-stroke oil' to mix with petrol in the two-stroke Saab 96s.

Competitions Department until the spring of 1962. Over the years, motorcycle manufacturers had already worked miracles with their two-stroke engines, and Saab certainly benefited from the build-up of knowledge gained, but the fact is that within the limitations of homologation it was very difficult for Saab ever to achieve more than about 80bhp from this 841cc engine. Until the triple Solex carburettor installation of the Sport came along in 1962, a peak 'works' power of about 65bhp was nearer the mark.

To quote from John Gott's 'Annual Review of International Rallying,' published in *Autosport* on 29 December 1961:

"The engine is perhaps the weakest part of the Saab. Whist completely reliable in Group 1 or Group 2 form, it is as yet markedly temperamental about pistons in Group 3 form, for Erik Carlsson had to retire with just that trouble in the [French] Alpine and the Liège, whilst a distributor packed up in the Tulip ..."

Homologated on 21 March 1960, the original 96 featured the standard three-speed gearbox, and (for Group 2) an alternative three-speeder, and two different four-speeders, whose internal ratios were:

Standard:
0.94, 1.57, 3.07, reverse 3.87:1

Alternatives:
0.96, 1.57, 3.17, reverse 3.87:1
0.84, 1.28, 2.10, 3.56, reverse 3.25 (or 2.92):1
0.84, 1.28, 2.09, 3.56, reverse 3.25 (or 2.92):1

The final drive ratio was 4.86:1, with 4.86, 5.14 and 5.43:1 all quoted as alternatives. At this point, too, I should repeat that the 96 had a transmission freewheel, which apparently had its advantages, and enabled gear-changing to be very fast at times. Incidentally, at no time was a centre-floor gear change even tested, and there seemed to be no pressure to abandon the steering column change with which all 96s and later V4s were equipped.

Amazingly, the rear suspension was quoted as 'Independent (Individuell),' which it was certainly not, for the beam axle system was like that of the 93 on which it had originally been introduced. Three different-sized fuel tanks – 36 litres, 60 litres and 95 litres – were all listed at first.

Even by 1961, little further improvement in performance was possible unless a different carburation system was adopted, so until the two-stroke-engined car gave way to the V4 in 1966/1967 the 'works' team had to concentrate on chassis improvements, and in making the car as ruggedly reliable as possible. With that in mind, a four-speed gearbox, and front-wheel disc brakes would surely be standardised for all markets.

Interestingly enough, no sooner had Erik Carlsson's

Saab 96 – why 96?

Here was a classic case of a project code making it to the showrooms, unchanged.
When Saab began the development of post-war aircraft, its first project was the Saab 90 (a civil airliner), and its second the Saab 91 (a training aircraft).
It therefore made sense that the Saab 92 code was applied to the original car, and that the Saab 93 was the model which replaced it. The original Sonett Super Sport sports car was Saab 94, the Estate car which came along in 1957 was the Saab 95 – so logically enough the car which took over from the 93 was the Saab 96 ...

car won the British RAC rally of 1961 than it was lent to *Autosport* magazine, where John Bolster duly broadcast his opinions on 5 January 1962. It is worth recalling that this car had run in a class appropriate to its specification, which included the four-speed gearbox. After quoting a top speed for this rally car of exactly 100mph, Bolster reminded his readership just how highly-tuned the engine was by noting that: "Not more than half-throttle may be employed below 3000rpm, and no worthwhile power is developed below 4000rpm ..."

When developing this car, in fact, Saab had achieved a remarkable transformation. Independent road tests of standard road cars showed that the 96 was only as brisk as the standard 850 Mini, with a top speed of 72mph, 0-60mph in a leisurely 26.6 seconds, and a standing-start quarter mile sprint in 23.5mph. The works rally car, on the other hand, achieved 100mph, 0-60mph in 14.8sec, and a standing quarter time in 19.6 seconds. In the rally car, third gear could whisk the car up to 70mph before fourth (top) gear was engaged. This was an astonishing improvement (Saab really knew its stuff when it came to power-tuning the two-stroke engine ...), and does a lot to explain why these cars could be so competitive in so many different environments.

Once again, to quote Bolster:

"One must pay attention when driving, to avoid giving too much throttle at low speeds. Once the engine is really revving the power output is tremendous. It 'comes in with a bang' and gives splendid acceleration, in spite of the considerable weight. The exhaust is so noisy that one fears prosecution, but the note builds up to a high scream that is music to the enthusiast's ear ..."

For weeks after this test was published, controversy raged in *Autosport's* Letters Page, with some writers claiming that the car had used a twin-choke carburettor, while Saab technicians insisted that it was the standard single-choke unit!

As already mentioned, the Saab 96 Sport appeared in February 1962, was homologated as soon as possible early in 1963, and was soon to be the weapon of choice in the works team, for the latest cars were significantly faster than before. From 1 July 1962, yet another choice of transmission (more rugged, to match the Sport engine) had been homologated:

0.92, 1.28, 1.86, 3.20, 2.92 (or 2.62):1

Allied to a low final drive ratio of 6.14:1

At the same time front-wheel disc brakes (standard on the Sport) were also approved on the original 'basic' 96. From 11 April 1964, yet more final drive ratios – 5.71:1 and 6.0:1 – were also approved, along with a Solex C44 P3I triple-choke carburettor, this being known internally as the 'Lancia carburettor' (from its original usage), and allowing the two-stroke to generate its ultimate peak horsepower.

Even though the technical limits had been reached, Saab spent much time then – and later – on tyre development with Dunlop and (not very seriously) with Goodyear. Contracts were not all-embracing in those days, which explains why Pirelli tyres were also used on occasion, along with some very strange studded rubber on Scandinavian winter events.

The fascia/instrument panel of the works-prepared 96 V4 of 1967 looked, and was, very simple. As on all these cars, the steering column gear-change was retained ...

It was with Dunlop, however, that Saab put in most effort on its winter-tyre development, which culminated in the evolution of extremely effective stud technology, and also resulted in very high-and-narrow profile covers for use in certain winter conditions where hard ice, rather than soft snow, was most prevalent. Much of the test driving was carried out by Swedish drivers living in Sweden – not because Erik Carlsson was incapable, but mainly because of the 1000km distance between Trollhättan and Tring in Hertfordshire.

By the mid-1960s, however, the cars, though always immaculately turned out, and as bravely driven as ever before, found their performance demonstrably lagging behind the opposition. They had reached the limits of two-stroke engine development, and the only way that more power could be achieved was by sacrificing the driveability of the package. The more work which went into the engines, the less flexible they became.

Simple statistics tell their own story – from 1963 to 1966, the Saab 96 Sport advanced very little, and seemed stuck with no more than about 75-80bhp. In the same period BMC's 'works' Mini-Coopers went from perhaps 80bhp to 110bhp, the 'works' Ford Cortinas moved up from 100bhp (Cortina GT) to 150bhp (Lotus-Cortina), and Porsche appeared with rear-engined 911s that produced up to 160bhp. In a simple power/weight ratio race, Saab was suffering.

This was where the arrival of the V4 seemed to solve many of Saab's rallying problems at a stroke. The new four-stroke model was homologated on 1 November 1966, and began its 'works' rallying career in February 1967, when it showed a great deal of promise. Normally-homologated machines were limited to the use of a single downdraught Solex carburettor, but, by mid-season, Group 5 cars with

... and even five years later the layout had not changed, though the trim was a little more elaborate ...

... but by 1976 there were more navigational fittings than ever before.

twin carbs had already been blooded, 1.7-litre versions producing up to 140bhp followed soon afterwards, and the race to develop more and more power was joined. Regulations, unhappily, meant that the Group 2 cars could run with only their standard 1.5-litre engines, and with standard inlet manifolds, but wherever it was possible in events with more liberal regulations, the larger/more powerful power units were employed.

The final homologation paper for the V4 was an impressive document, for Saab carried forward everything that had been useful on two-stroke cars (if it was still suitable for the new model) and added many more novelties.

This shows how short and compact the front end of the 96 and V4 models actually was. Taken in 1969, it shows the initial build up of the V4 which Erik Carlsson would take on the Baja 1000 event.

Apart from the use of the new engine, there had been a rethink of transmissions, both of which were four-speeders:

0.84, 1.30, 2.09, 3.48, reverse 3.18:1
0.92, 1.30, 1.86, 3.14, reverse 2.87:1

Allied to these final drive ratios: 4.89, 5.14, 5.43, 5.71.

A further final drive ratio – 6.01 – was homologated from 1 April 1967, and 5.83: followed in July 1967.

From January 1968, yet another set of ratios was also homologated, in a revised and sturdier cast iron casing:

0.92, 1.19, 1.60, 2.64, 2.08:1

At the same time, a cam-and-pawl limited-slip diff was also homologated into Group 2. These were part of a

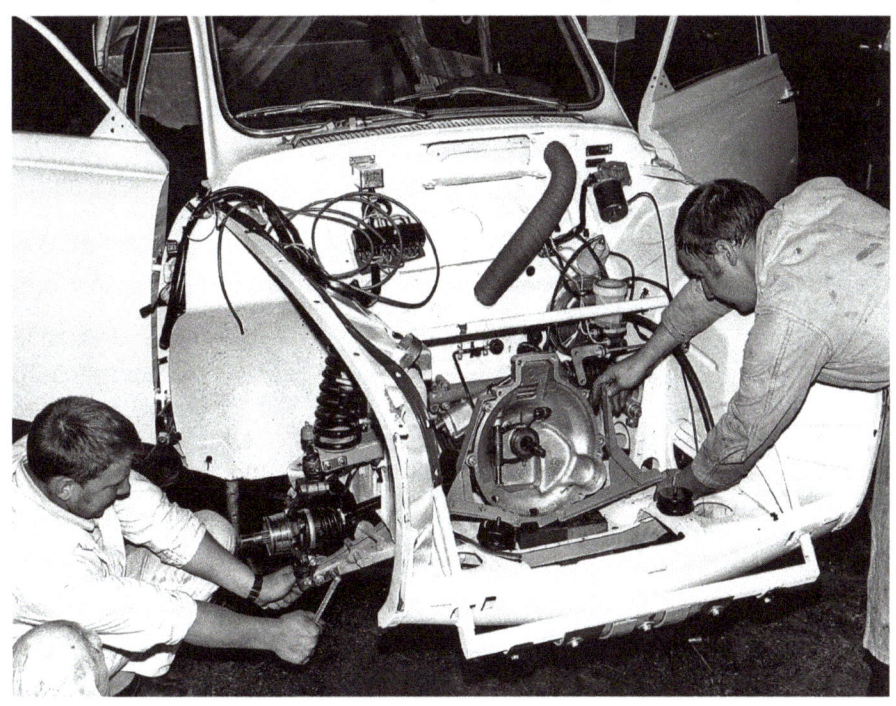

Ford-Germany V4 engine

It is important to stress that although Ford-UK and Ford-Germany were both wholly-owned subsidiaries of the American giant Ford Motor Co., technically, the companies were not linked until 1967 – when Ford-of-Europe was set up, and the two concerns rapidly merged. Until that moment, each company effectively ran its own design, engineering and development functions, though there was considerable 'influence' from the USA in matters concerning styling, and in general mechanical layouts.

Accordingly, it was no coincidence that both European subsidiaries developed new families of V4 and V6 engines in the 1960s, and it was certainly no coincidence that the two engine families were totally un-related in detail.

As described in the main text, the replacement of its existing two-stroke engine was first considered by Saab in 1962, and the decision to buy-in an engine (rather than develop a new power unit of its own) came in 1963. Many European engines were considered, the contract finally going to Ford-Germany.

The original Ford-Cologne V4 engine was announced in 1962, a 1183cc/40bhp power unit. The 1498cc engine soon followed (it was originally rated at 50bhp), and by the end of the 1960s, the ultimate stretch was of 1698cc/75bhp (as used in the original Ford Capri, and high-powered Taunus 15M/17M family cars). Both the larger capacity units would be used in Saab V4s.

This family of engines powered a whole variety of Ford cars, including the iconic Transit van, and was built in millions before being phased out in the late 1970s. All engines supplied to Saab were produced in the Ford-Germany/Ford-Europe engine plant close to Cologne, in Germany.

It must be stressed that this family of Ford-Germany V4s had absolutely no technical links with the Ford-of-Britain V4s that were produced in the 1960s and 1970s.

---

definite move toward a dedicated Group 2 specification, making the cars even more suitable for (I surmise) tarmac rallying and circuit racing, for this was indeed a close-ratio set.

At first, in any case, to run the V4s in fully-tuned non-homologated form put unsupportable amounts of stress into the transmission which often led to gear or even casing failure, but by mid-1968 the latest cast iron casing had been further developed, and seemed to help to alleviate that problem. The same new gearbox casing could also house a limited-slip differential (Saab had not previously used such a fitment) which, when used on the RAC rally, gave trouble, and caused Tom Trana's retirement, though the other two cars (driven by Lampinen and Orrenius) dominated the event throughout.

Unhappily, by 1968 the cars were already lagging behind their new rivals in performance terms. To quote pundit John Davenport:

"Second in the Constructors' Championship was the Saab V4, and while it is fascinating to see that no fewer than 23 of its 36 points were scored by Simo Lampinen, it is also nice to see one of the Grand Old Factories of European rallying showing that they can still win events with a car that is much slower than its opposition. It is a shame that this car should be underpowered, but the Saab factory is so reluctant to indulge itself by producing a sports version with a string of homologated goodies that it has no-one to blame but itself ..."

It was the same story, but more so, in 1969, even when a Borg Warner limited-slip differential was homologated.

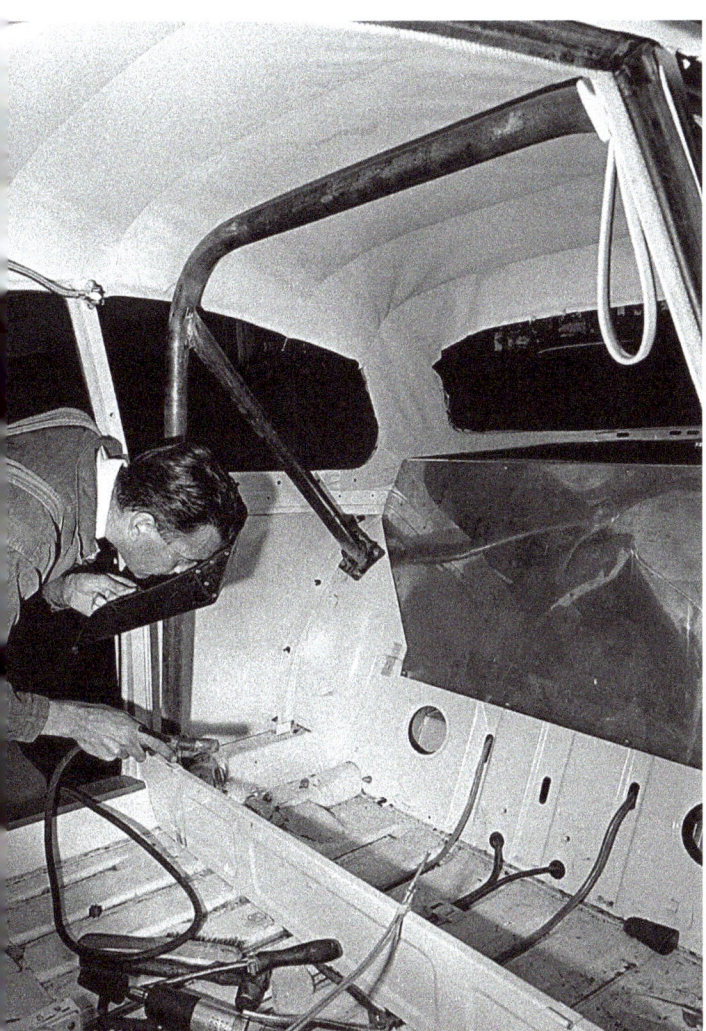

Saab was quite late in adding roll cages to its rally cars. This is preparation of one of the cars built to tackle the Baja 1000 race of 1969.

This was just one of several nose treatments applied to the V4. In 1974 square headlamps were fitted to some cars ...

... while circular headlamps were fitted to USA-market models.

Although bravely driven, the cars were increasingly outpaced, and though the V4 engines produced a little (unspecified) more power than before, the transmission seemed to have increasing difficulties in coping with this. Most 'works' cars had the very latest rectangular headlamp noses, but not until the factory's stocks of old models had been used up. Coping

Sturdy Recaro seats like this were fitted to the factory-prepared V4s in the 1960s and 1970s.

with inevitable weight increases was always a challenge, especially when steel roll-over bars, which later became more comprehensive, were adopted. The first usage of such bars, it seems, was in the Baja event of 1969 which, although a publicity-conscious irrelevance in motorsport terms, did great things for Saab's sporting image in the USA.

Lampinen, for instance, won the non-Championship 1969 Scottish in an old round-headlamp car, this also being a Group 6 machine with many lightweight panels and 'glass'! Those lightweight panels (thin steel in the doors) and glass-fibre wings, bonnet, etc – allied to Plexiglass door, rear quarter and rear window 'glass' – were homologated from 1 January 1970. It was at about this time that the department was able to acquire the occasional special body shell from the production lines, which had been strengthened in some ways, and with a number of details (under-sealing, padding of trim, and related items) deleted; such shells could also be supplied to carefully chosen private drivers.

The next big change for the rally team came in 1971, and there was absolutely no subterfuge involved. For the 1971 model year, where cars sold in the USA

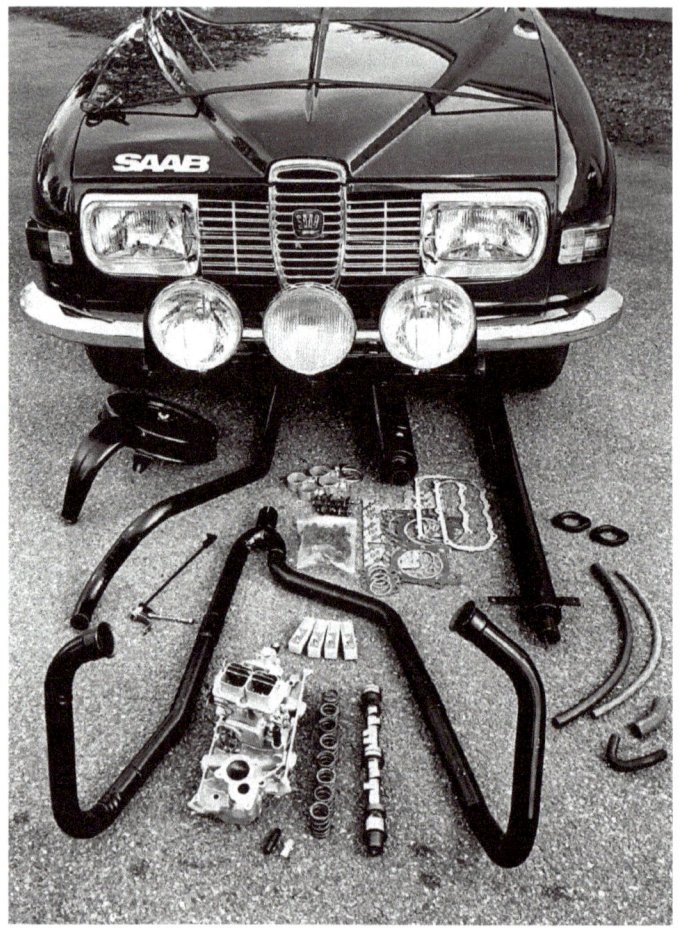

By 1973, Saab had developed a large range of extra competition parts for the V4.

tended to have their engines 'strangled' by new emissions control regulations, manufacturers usually responded

By the early 1970s, Saab had super-tuned the V4 engine to use twin, opposed, dual-choke Weber carburettors. Simo Lampinen won the 1972 1000 Lakes event using this particular engine.

By the mid-1970s, the engine bay of the 1.8-litre Group 2 cars looked extremely tidy. By this time the team cars were using the final 'dual exhaust port' cylinder heads.

V4 engine preparation in 1975, showing the final type of cylinder head, which featured twin exhaust outlets (instead of the single outlet used on earlier cars).

by increasing the size of engines used. Accordingly, for 1971, and with USA-spec road cars being sold with 1.7-litre engines (same cylinder bore as before, but a longer stroke, and therefore more mid-speed torque); new sets of homologation papers (No. 1608 – dated 1 January 1971) were produced, and the team cars made a significant advance.

From this point, in almost all cases, they would run with 1740cc engines, occasionally 1815cc, and would eventually

This was an early version of the fuel injection system that was tried out on the V4 engine at the end of the 1960s.

settle on a Group 2 specification which involved the use of two twin-choke Weber carburettors with cross-over inlet manifolds. In addition, certain other changes and more relaxed provisions in some homologation rules had allowed the V4s to be tried with fuel injection, though this was eventually set aside. Power outputs of 150bhp-155bhp were quoted, which might have made the cars totally competitive if this had been available in 1968, but not nearly so two years later on, in 1970.

This, incidentally, put quite a strain on the transmissions, which seemed to break much more often than in previous seasons, even though a further-strengthened casing was

Power outputs – road cars

The following table shows how Saab 96-family and V4 power outputs increased over the years:

Year	Model	Engine size (cc)	Peak power
1960	96	841cc 2-str	38bhp
1960	96 GT750	748cc 2-str	45bhp
1962	96 Sport/Monte Carlo	841cc 2-str	55bhp
1966	Sonett II (94) Coupé	841cc 2-str	60bhp
1966	96 V4	1498cc 4-str	65bhp
1969	Sonett III (97) Coupé	1698cc 4-str	65bhp

homologated on 1 January 1971. Transmission failures tended to be quite random, too – differentials, output shafts, and driveshafts all suffering their (unwanted) share of failures. As already explained, there was little the team could do about this, and the drivers lived in constant dread of a random failure.

It didn't help that a new type of modified cylinder head, which breathed more deeply than before and liberated even more torque, was tried out on prototype Group 5 cars in 1972, and which would then be homologated in July 1973, came on stream. This featured twin exhaust port outlets in each head, rather than the single port on original production cars, and was made by ruthlessly machining back the existing casting, to eliminate the siamesed junction, then welding a new twin-port adaptor into place. Such heads were then matched to a developed version of the cross-manifold/twin-choke Weber carburettor installation.

With up to 170bhp now claimed, this put an even greater strain on the front-wheel drive transmission. The search for stronger gearboxes always continued, but within the limits of the existing casing little could now be done. By the end of 1973, however, Saab had finally started using Salisbury limited-slip differentials as an alternative to the Borg Warner units which had previously figured in these cars.

Towards the very end of the V4's life, Saab (with, it must be stressed, some help from Ford-Germany, which built the road-car engines), managed to produce a very limited number of large-bore cylinder blocks (which carried a bore dimension of 96mm), this being done by altering the internal casting details of the block as much as was practical. This pushed the engine's cubic capacity to no less than 1933cc, and for which peak power was 175bhp. In 1975 this engine gave encouraging results in local Scandinavian events, but there was always the likelihood that it would chew up the already over-stressed transmissions. Saab, for sure, did not tell the world that it was using different cylinder block castings (which would not have been sporting legal). However, as was the case with the conversion of Ford Escort RS1800s from 1.85 litres to full 2-litre machines, there was no need to have this capacity homologated, as it was still within the same 2-litre class.

After this, 96 V4 rally car development ceased, as the factory transferred all its attention to the new-generation 99 range. The V4 which Per Eklund drove to victory in the Swedish KAK rally of February 1976 was no stronger, and certainly no more powerful, than any other 'works' Saab prepared in the previous three years.

Were the Saab 96 (and the V4) unique?

It is only fair to say that, as an engineering package, the 96/V6 family was not unique, but when it was linked to stupendously gifted rally drivers like Erik Carlsson, Simo Lampinen and Stig Blomqvist, the combination most certainly was unique. Even so, at the height of its powers as a two-stroke-engined car, the combination of excellent (for its engine size) power, excellent handling and front-wheel-drive packaging, all allied to the very robust body shell, was very appealing to private owners.

Except in very rare cases where rallies were settled on sprint/hill-climb/handicap formulae, where small-engined Auto Unions and DKWs could be competitive, the 96 was the only two-stroke-engined rally car to be competitive on a pan-European basis. Naturally, a Saab was expected to win in Scandinavia, and in British events using the same special-stage/loose-surface formula, but no-one, surely, could have expected to see a 96 winning in Eastern Europe, or in true marathons such as Spa-Sofia-Liège.

Because the 96 was at its peak at the same time as the BMC Mini-Cooper S, private owners without any national, dealership or sponsorship ties sometimes found it difficult to choose between the two brands. The records, in fact, show that the majority of 96 rally cars were driven by Scandinavians, and that Mini-Cooper S cars tended to be bought and rallied by individuals in Britain, Europe and the old 'Empire' countries like South Africa and Australia.

Building and running the 'works' cars

As already mentioned, the early 'works' cars were prepared in the general test and engineering development departments, but the official Competitions Department was set up in Trollhättan, to be managed by Bosse Hellberg, in March 1962, and with later-well-known technicians Pelle Rudh and Sven Olsson leading the mechanics. From this point, the team broke free of mainstream engineering, and had its own modest workshops in Trollhättan. By 1965 it had moved once again to a small but purpose-built complex, complete with engine test bed facilities. Critically, this was outside the main activities of Saab, which meant that, when the chips were down, things could go ahead at a more frantic pace than would be normal in a big department.

This is the 'works' Competition Workshop in transition, in 1974, with evidence of much work on the new-type 99, as well as the V4s.

Even when Erik Carlsson was joined by his new wife Pat Moss in the team for 1964, the fleet of factory rally cars was also limited, as the basic body structure was very solid, so it was usually possible to rebuild a car even after some of the more arduous events. Those were the days in which Hellberg could call on the services of his assistants, Bo Swaner, one secretary, and a team of technicians (mainly mechanics, along with one engine specialist) who totalled no more than about twenty people at first. On a major event like Monte Carlo, therefore, there would only be three or four service crews (all of them in Saab 95 Estate cars), and perhaps a van carrying wheels and tyres – and yet although this sounds like penny-pinching, it was none-the-less a very effective 'umbrella.'

Before then, rally cars had been built, rebuilt, and developed within the main development department of the company, so many links – especially with the engine and transmissions specialists – were retained for many years. In those days the fleet of rally cars was always very restricted – the 96 family was very rugged, so did not require massive rebuilds after every event – perhaps two or three cars for

Erik Carlsson's Monte-winning 96 of 1962 had the simplest of fascias/instrument displays.

each of the star drivers. So, along with back-up cars and the occasional test car, perhaps no more than ten rally cars at any one time. The stock of engines, also, was extremely limited, though one or two units would often be found working on test beds, with future power and torque increases in mind. Service cars, of course, were also maintained by the same enthusiastic team.

"Normally we ran cars as long as they lasted," Bo Swaner

The entire staff of the Competitions Department, as grouped around a V4 rally car in 1970.

major characters. On events, or in the workshop, Erik would ask mechanics to make particular changes, and they would do that, without ever having to refer it to Bosse Hellberg or Bo Swaner.

The legend goes that very few people at Saab knew a lot about the V4-engine transplant project which resulted in the Saab 96 V4 – not, that is, until a few months before the change over took place. The 'works' competitions department, for sure, did not, so it had to learn all about four-stroke engines, V4 engines in particular, at very short notice, in 1966/1967. No behind-the-scenes testing had been carried out before the new model went public.

Mention Saab V4 rally cars to any Saab enthusiast, and they will agree that the transmission was the aspect of the car which had the toughest task, especially

told me, "and unless they had a big accident, with engine/transmission changes, they might last for one or even two years. Later, as the cars got more complicated, we changed them more often."

Even so (and especially as the V4 programme progressed), the team still found time to build cars for private owners, or for Saab concessionaires overseas – maybe five or six every year. Saab, gentlemanly as ever, saw this as one way of generating income, to help lift the modest budget a little!

In the early two-stroke era of the 96, this was definitely 'Erik's team,' which quite smoothly became 'Erik and Pat's team' when the husband and wife combination took over. It was not until Erik retired from driving, and Pat moved to Lancia, that other world-class drivers like Ove Andersson, Simo Lampinen, Åke Andersson and Stig Blomqvist became

on the later cars where 175bhp (and occasionally more) was being fed through the same casing as normal V4s. Mainstream engineering helped where it could, especially regarding heat treatment, material thicknesses, and other details, but there was no way that the same physical package could really be expected to withstand the torque of a 175bhp rally car engine indefinitely!

In 1969, a few years after the 96 V4 had gone into production, Saab set up a joint company with OY Valmet AB, in Finland, which led to assembly of those cars at a factory at Uusikaupunki. Originally, the cars were built up from CKD (Completely Knocked Down) kits manufactured at Trollhättan, but more and more pieces were eventually manufactured in Finland.

Soon after this, the Finns set up their own 'satellite' rally team under Robbie Grorndahl. The team prepared its own cars (with some components – notably engines – provided from Trollhättan), hired its own Finnish drivers (such as Simo Lampinen and Tapio Rainio), and started entering events in Scandinavia (and occasionally the British RAC rally). The Swedes were delighted about this, not only because the cars and drivers were demonstrably the equal of their own, but because the Finns provided their own finance. Not only that, but the Finns seemed to be happiest when they were beating the Swedes!

Although the cars were mechanically identical to the Swedish 'works' cars, they were visually special, being mainly white and blue, as opposed to the familiar red the Swedish 'works' cars carried. This operation ran until the late 1970s, but closed down as the 96 V4 programme ended, for the Finnish team was not as committed to 99s or Turbos: assembly of 96 V4 road cars continued in Finland, in fact, until 1980.

After the world rally team closed, the staff and mechanics were dispersed to take up other jobs in the organisation, though contact with motorsport was never totally lost. Saab continued to be successful in rallycross for some years, for example, and there were official (and even unofficial!) ways for its drivers to tap into the growing expertise of the engineers.

Personalities and star drivers

Before giving detail of several individual careers, it is worth mentioning that in the earlier years, Scandinavian Saab drivers sometimes shone at home, but rarely ventured south of the Baltic Sea. Nevertheless, at home the superstars really were stellar, and all are respected to this day.

Bosse Hellberg

At the start of his career, Bosse Hellberg had worked with the KAK (the equivalent, really, of the British RAC) in Sweden, whose responsibilities included running the Midnight Sun Rally. He had already become known as a rallying co-driver in Sweden.

Bo Hellberg headed the Saab competitions department throughout its life, and saw the 96 evolve from an under-powered two-stroke car to a much more competitive 1.8-litre machine.

Hellberg became Saab's competition manager when the 'works' team took up its separate existence in 1962, and stayed in that position until it pulled out of world level motorsport in the early 1980s. It was Hellberg, along with Saab's PR department (who provided most of the budget), and who set the programme every year. Hellberg, who became known as something of an 'Old Fox,' recognised those events good for his cars, and those which were not. This explains, for sure, why Scandinavian events could be linked to the British RAC, and to Monte Carlo, for all of them suited front-wheel-drive machinery.

After staying at the helm of the motorsport activity until 1981 when the department was closed, he took over the running of the mainstream quality control department, and became very dedicated to that job.

Bo Swaner

Looking ridiculously young when appointed, and still remarkably spry when the department closed, Bo Swaner joined the Saab Competitions department as Bosse Hellberg's assistant in 1964. Having been a rally co-driver, and knowing Gunnar Palm, he was offered that job, and took it up just as soon as he had finished his academic studies (mechanical engineering) in mid-season! Bo then stayed with the 'works' team until it closed, later taking more senior positions in the mainstream factory's technical workshops.

Like Gunnar Palm, who he resembled in some ways, Swaner was always the fresh-faced, ever-helpful contact the media had with the Saab team. He combined his great enthusiasm for the sport with a detailed knowledge of homologation and rallies all round the world, and, along with Bo Hellberg, much of the changes and advances made on these cars were to his credit. Although there was never a major shake-up in the organisation, by the 1970s Swaner had taken on more and more responsibilities, and had become Team Manager.

From 1978, Bo moved out of motorsport, taking over as project leader for the new Saab 900 project, while it was being tested in the USA, after which he took over management of the mainstream technical and development laboratories at Trollhättan. Later in life, Swaner remained with Saab, reaching director level, before retiring, going

Bo Swaner was Bo Hellberg's much-respected assistant in the Saab 'works' rally team during the 1960s and 1970s, eventually becoming the de facto Team Manager.

into politics, and becoming involved in motorsport at world level.

Erik Carlsson

A Saab driver from the 1950s until he retired in 1967, and a company spokesman for the next thirty years, Erik is the most

Posed for advertising purposes, this was Erik 'on the roof' Carlsson, with a beached 96, drowning his sorrows in a bottle of Pommac beer.

famous of all Saab rally drivers – and rightly so. Born in 1929 at Trollhättan (the home of Saab), Erik first rallied a Saab 92 in 1952, became Western District Champion of Sweden in 1954, and took his first truly major rally victory in the 1000 Lakes event of 1957 (in a Saab 93). In the meantime, he was employed by Saab as a test and development driver, so was already well-known inside the company before rallying became all-important to him.

By the end of the decade Erik rivalled Carl-Magnus Skogh as Saab's leading rally driver, as successful in Europe as he was in his native Scandinavia. By this time he had rolled enough rally cars to gain the nickname 'på taket' (on the roof) – derived from a Swedish children's cartoon character 'Karlsson på taket' (who lived on the roof of an apartment building), though eventually he outlived this.

After narrowly failing to win the European Rally

Erik Carlsson, the great man himself. In the 1950s and 1960s, Erik was not only Saab's best rally driver, but probably the world's, too.

Championship in 1959 (a penalty for car body damage on the final event in Portugal was his undoing), he cemented his reputation for all time with two Monte Carlo and three RAC victories, along with Midnight Sun, 1000 Lakes, Acropolis, German and San Remo successes, plus any number of phenomenal performances in events as diverse as the East African Safari, the French Alpine, and the Spa-Sofia-Liège. It was only a chronic and worsening back problem (caused by the battering of many high jumps in rallies) that caused him to retire from serious motorsport in the late 1960s.

Erik was a big man in all respects – with a massive physique, a massive personality, and enormous driving talents.

Two generations of famous Saab rally drivers – left-to-right: Stig Blomqvist, Erik Carlsson and Per Eklund.

Dominant in a car (he liked to get his own way, emphatically, as nervous co-drivers soon found out ...), he imposed his will on its handling and performance at all times, achieving the most astonishing results against all normal expectations.

It was often said that Erik invented 'left-foot-braking,' to get the very best out of his Saabs with limited power outputs, though his dislike for using the brakes in all but the most dire necessity was well-known. When asked why he seemed to take his Saab over any blind brow apparently without lifting off the throttle, Erik retorted: 'Well, road must go somewhere ..."

Not only was he a peerless driver, but he soon mastered enough English to provide a stream of quotable quotes, but only to media personnel whom he trusted.

Having met Pat Moss (see below) in European motorsport in the late 1950s, the two rapidly became inseparable whenever rallying commitments allowed it – when Erik was not driving Saabs in events, he was often to be seen driving BMC 'chase cars' at the time – and they were married in July 1963. Erik then moved to England to be with Pat. The marriage was successful, and after Erik retired from competitive sport, he became a world-wide ambassador for Saab, all the time giving in gracefully to Pat's renewed enthusiasm for equestrianism.

Even after his rallying days were long gone, Erik would occasionally take out a 'works' Saab in front of the media, and set incredibly competitive times on special stages in testing. Even in the 1970s, when alighting from cars like the 99 Turbo, on such occasions, he would ease his creaking back, grin, and then quip: "Not bad ... for old man ..."

Pat Moss

Everyone loved Pat Moss. I have never found anyone with a word to say against her. Although she arrived in rallying in 1955 with the damning phrase of 'Stirling's little sister' hanging around her neck, within five years of joining the BMC team, she had not only become a credible lady rally driver, but had actually won the toughest of all rallies outright (the Liège-Sofia-Liège) in an Austin-Healey 3000.

By that time there was no doubt that this slight, devastatingly pretty, and (outwardly only) insecure young lady had become an established member of the team. Although she seemed to be scatter-brained to a fault (she left her handbag behind at hotels, restaurants, and rally service points many times!), and liked to trade on the 'wide-eyed innocent' reputation that developed over time, she was, nevertheless, ferociously competitive, with great endurance and a real will to win.

Once she came to terms with the Big Healey (she always said it frightened her, but then, Paddy Hopkirk had said the same thing – and they both won events in the cars) she was often as fast as all but the two Flying Finns, and was already being measured, and compared, on a daily basis, by all her peers. Though broad-shouldered, with enough body strength to cope with these big cars, Pat was strictly the sort of active, sport-loving lady who disarmed most men with her charm – yet she could also become depressed if the cars were not always in good health. Converting to Mini-Coopers was surprisingly straightforward – she became competitive at once – and really flew the Mini-Cooper flag in the only season (1962) in which she drove them. The workshop staff at Abingdon was almost ready to walk through flame to build her a good example of any rally car.

Each of her cars got nicknames (her Liège-winning Healey, URX 727, was soon known as 'Uurrxx,' her long-lived Morris 1000 was 'Granny,' while a singularly unlucky Healey 3000 was always known as 'The Thing'), and, of course, she had her own foibles about equipment. Like big brother Stirling, she liked her car registration numbers, and competition numbers, to have a '7' in them – but she disliked the number '13.'

Having met the mountainous Swedish rally driver Erik Carlsson in 1959, the two rapidly became an item, not only in rallying but in private life, and Pat eventually married Erik in July 1963 to become, officially, Pat Moss-Carlsson. For 1963 she moved from BMC to Ford-UK, and for 1964, both she and Erik were courted by Ford (who offered big financial incentives, which Saab could not match).

Instead of Erik joining her at Ford, she decided to join Erik at Saab, and enjoyed four seasons with the Trollhättan team. Pat, like Erik, loved the way the 96 handled, and took every advantage of its rugged strength, but after her years of

Together from the late 1950s, and married in 1963, Pat Moss and Erik Carlsson not only shared a happy life, but were both extremely successful in motorsport. Erik was, of course, 'Mr Saab' for many years, while Pat drove for the rally team in the 1960s.

driving 210bhp Austin-Healeys, the lack of power (if not of traction) must have felt frustrating at times.

From 1968, though, she moved once again, to drive with Lancia, but she was never seen as a total icon for those teams, not in the same way that she had always been at BMC.

When she died in 2008, there was general sadness in motorsport, for lady drivers of her calibre were, and are, very thin on the ground.

Carl-Magnus Skogh

To quote John Gott in 1961: "Carl-Magnus Skogh is little-known outside Scandinavia, but if he seriously attempted to win the Championship title, he would be a very hard man to beat. For several years now he has finished well up in the Championship field, usually amassing his points in a very few events. In the four rallies he ran in, he won the Midnight Sun, was second in the Tulip and the Polish, and fourth in the 1000 Lakes, a typical result of his extremely fast, consistent, driving ..."

Born in 1925, Skogh, in fact, did not start rallying until he was 25 years old, but had already been at the top of the Swedish rallying tree for years by 1961. He won the Norwegian Viking rally (in a Saab 93) as early as 1956 (he won it three times in all), won the Swedish rally in 1960 and 1961, and was, it seemed, the equal of Erik Carlsson by this time. In the limited surroundings of Saab, perhaps, there were now too many superstars in one place, and at the age of 37 Skogh therefore accepted an offer from Volvo, to become one of the stars in its rally team.

In the next few years Skogh pedalled the heavy, but definitely nimble, Volvo Amazons, as fast as any other driver in the world, won events like the Greek Acropolis, and even after retirement from rallying he stayed behind at Volvo, until the end of his working life.

Simo Lampinen

Throughout his years in top-class rallying, Simo always looked much too young for his task, had a disarming smile, impeccable manners, and an impressive command of the English language – all allied to great natural ability as a rally driver.

Born at Porvoo in Finland in 1943, to a prosperous family whose business made skis and other gear, Simo was originally intent on becoming a Finnish ski jumping champion. Then, unhappily, he contracted polio while in his early teens, which ended his ski jumping ambitions, and although he happily recovered, this left him with a rather lumbering, lurching and somehow unnerving gait. The story goes that, when asked to approve a driving contract, one company boss who did not know him, thought that he might have been signing up a disabled driver, but a quick demonstration drive soon changed his mind ...

Instead of skiing, Simo took up rallying within days of gaining a driving licence, and proved that he had remarkable skills in privately-prepared (then Finnish-supported) Saab 96s, this included winning the Finnish 1000 Lakes rallies of 1963 and 1964 before that was a European Championship event. In the same years he also became Finnish rally champion, after which the world of motoring sat up and took notice, and his fame soon spread across the world. He joined Triumph for 1965, but was cast adrift when that marque withdrew from rallying in 1966, and he finally joined the Saab 'works' team in 1967.

Carl-Magnus Skogh was one of the most formidable performers in the two-stroke 96, winning several major international events until he was head-hunted by Volvo.

When Erik Carlsson gave up rallying at this level, Simo became one of the team's leading lights, but was eventually tempted away by the promise of mountains of Italian money to join the Lancia team (driving Fulvia HFs and Beta Coupés) instead. Over the course of the next decade he drove other Lancias, Fiat 131 Abarths, Saab V4s, Triumph TR7 V8s and Peugeot 504 V6 Coupés, before finally retiring to become a much-respected motorsport administrator. For years he was Clerk of the Course of the 1000 Lakes (later known as the Neste) rally, and in the 2000s was often seen in a major officiating capacity up to world level.

Stig Blomqvist

Although Stig Blomqvist probably drove more rally cars, in more years, than any of his rivals, he originally made his name behind the wheel of front-wheel-drive Saabs. Although his first major result came as early as 1967 (Saab 96 V4), and his last Saab success (99 Turbo) came in 1982, he became World Rally Champion in 1984 (Audi Quattro), and last competed at World Championship level in 2006.

Born in Orebro (Sweden) in 1946, he began rallying

Stig Blomqvist, seen here with an early 99 Turbo, was a stalwart member of the Saab rally team throughout the 1970s.

Stig Blomqvist (left) was Saab's rally team leader throughout the 1970s, winning events in both V4s and in 99s, while Bjorn Cederberg became his co-driver.

in 1964 when still only 18 years of age (naturally using a Saab 96), became a 'works' driver at the end of the 1960s, and rapidly became the de facto team leader of this tight-knit little Swedish organisation. Although his character was totally different from Saab's previous hero, Erik Carlsson, Stig built up a large following – deservedly so.

His first big victory came in 1971 (RAC rally), and by 1978 he'd also won the Swedish rally four times in V4s, going on to be the only 'works' driver who truly tamed the much bigger and more powerful Saab 99 and Turbo family. On the other hand, he probably rolled more Saabs than any of his contemporaries – but this was probably because he was usually going faster than all of them, and competing in more events.

Amiable but taciturn (he could be a near-silent nightmare to interview, unless he knew and respected his

Stig Blomqvist (left) and Arne Hertz – love that T-shirt!

questioner), he later developed a particularly attractive sing-song 'Stinglish,' loved Britain so much that he eventually bought a home in London, and spent his prime years in rally cars as diverse as the Audi Quattro, the Ford RS200, and the Nissan Sunny GTI-R. To those engineers who could persuade him to say more than a few words, he also proved to be a patient and deep-thinking test/development driver, who loved rallying so much that he kept on competing, even at Historic and rally show demonstration level, until he was approaching pensionable age.

Like a few (by no means many) drivers, one could put him into a strange car and almost immediate see him coax astonishing stage times out of it. Examples of this came in 1996, when he finished third in Britain's RAC rally in a Skoda Felicia 'kit car,' and in 2000, when he won the Historic London-Sydney Marathon Rally in a Ford Capri Perana V8.

In many ways he always was, and remains, the most popular driver in historic motorsport too.

A young Stig Blomqvist, in 1973, with fashionably long hair.

Per Eklund

Although Per Eklund does not have a totally stellar reputation in rallying (not, that is, in terms of statistics), he was a solid, dependable and altogether essential member of the Saab 'works' team for some years. Born in Skonnerud in Sweden, in 1946, 'Pekka' started rallying in the late 1960s, and first broke into the Saab 'works' team in 1970. Until Saab reduced its rally programme after the arrival of the new-generation 99 model, Eklund and Stig Blomqvist were two of the most durable characters in the 'works' line-up.

Having won the Norwegian Winter rally twice – in 1969 and 1971 – Per then spread his wings to other events outside Scandinavia, and set a whole series of fine performances, until he won the Swedish rally of 1976. Number crunchers

In the 1970s Per Eklund became one of the stalwarts of the 'works' Saab rally team. After the rally team was disbanded he not only performed valiantly for other marques, but also won many rallycross events in Saabs.

will want to know that Per's first and only world win was also the last to be recorded by a Saab V4 – the Swedish KAK in February 1976 ...

Like his team-mate, Stig Blomqvist (were they rivals? Perhaps, but neither seems to have made a point of it), Per never uttered two sentences to the media if a single sentence would provide the same opinions, but his open and cheerful attitude to rallying was admired by all of us in the media.

He was Swedish Rally Champion in 1978, but once Saab released him he went on to drive for Austin-Rover (Triumph TR7 V8), for Toyota, and later in privately-financed Audi Quattros. He also became a formidably successful rallycross driver, finishing second in the 1998, 2002 and 2003 European Rallycross Championships.

Per Eklund joined the Saab 'works' team in the early 1970s, and was soon considered the equal of Stig Blomqvist in identical cars.

Competition story

The 'works' Saab's career

Although Saab had originally dabbled in rallying with the sweet but drastically underpowered 92 (even in fully-developed 'works' form the twin-cylinder 764cc engine produced only about 35bhp), the cars did not become credible, or competitive, until the three-cylinder/748cc 93 model appeared in 1956. It was from 1960, however, that the team became serious, with the arrival of the 96.

Homologated within weeks of public announcement, the 841cc car soon made its mark.

1960

Immediately after it was homologated in March 1960, the 96's very first appearance at major European level came in April, when Erik Carlsson tried out the new car on the Geneva, but without success.

Just four weeks later, in early May, when two cars – for Carlsson (modified) and Carl Orrenius (a standard car) – appeared on the Tulip rally, it was a different story. Although this event started and finished in Holland, much of the competitors' time was spent charging up and down hills in France; all the way to Monte Carlo and back, in fact. The very tight time schedules with different 'handicap' timings favoured the smaller-engined cars, as *The Autocar's* reporter noted when observing on the Col des Leques:

"Particularly impressive here were the two-stroke-engined cars, Auto Unions and Saabs. Holding the same gear between the acute corners, the buzz of their motors, cutting in and out for the bends, could be heard a long way down the hill. One exception was Erik Carlsson, who appeared to be taking everything on full throttle ..."

This, of course, was a phenomenon serious rallying observers had already noted, and was a characteristic that would remain with the towering colossus of Scandinavian motorsport for many years to come.

Only eight cars kept to the demanding road-car schedule, but two of them were the Saabs, and after all the handicaps had diligently been worked out, Carl Orrenius took second place overall, Carlsson was sixth, and both cars won their respective classes.

Two weeks later the redoubtable Carlsson/Karlsson combination repeated the trick in another 96, this time in the hot, rough, and dusty conditions of the Acropolis rally in Greece. On this occasion, they were beaten only by Walter Shock (already on his way to winning the European Championship), in his fuel-injected Mercedes-Benz 220SE. In a way, though, the Tulip and the Acropolis were just the curtain raisers for what was to follow. In June, August and September, the still-new 96 chalked up three outright victories and three second places, all with the same modest but highly-tuneable two-stroke engine, a three-speed steering-column gear change, and drum brakes!

In June, where the Midnight Sun rally was made up entirely of gravel-surfaced special stages, it was Carl-Magnus Skogh's car that beat the entire field, including a fleet of Volvos, and no less than Gunnar Bengtsson in a high-performance Porsche 356. It was on high-speed, flowing stages like this, where bravery and a smooth driving style, all allied to experience, could make up for power deficiencies.

Carl-Magnus Skogh on the Norwegian Viking Rally of 1960; an early outing for the Saab 96.

One of the first events that Saab came to dominate was the Swedish Midnight Sun, where front-wheel-drive and brave drivers were the winning combination. This was Carl-Magnus Skogh.

The first of many 1000 Lakes victories for the Saab 96. Carl Otto Bremer (right) and Juhani Lampi won the event in 1960.

The same conditions, and the same desirable technique, applied to the Finnish 1000 Lakes in August. The same superstars (the 'usual suspects,' one might say) turned out, and once again this was more-or-less a head-to-head fight between two Swedish marques – Saab and Volvo. In the end not one, but three, Saabs headed the lists – Bremer, Erik Carlsson and Carl-Magnus Skogh in that order – with Gunnar Andersson's Volvo hot on their heels. It was the same story in Norway just four weeks later, but on that occasion Skogh's Saab won the event outright – which meant that Saab had made a clean sweep of all three Scandinavian events in the 1960 European series.

Then came the climax of the 1960 season, the British RAC rally, where Erik Carlsson turned up in a single 'works' 96, determined to make amends for 1959, when he had retired after burying his 93 in a wall in a Welsh village. This time, one might say, it was personal, for British navigational expert Stuart Turner was drafted in to look after the co-driving side, and the format of the event could not have been more ideal for this duo. Much of the event, particularly in the Pennines

A famous occasion. This was the 1960 RAC rally, where Erik Carlsson started from the very back of the field in his 96, but was the only driver to be unpenalised on the four special stages. His co-driver was Stuart Turner. The two are seen here at a time control talking to Motor Sport *editor Bill Boddy.*

on the first night, and in Wales on the last night, was navigational, where it was all too easy to lose time, but way up in the north of Scotland the event included the first four special stages ever to be incorporated in a British International.

The very first stage, over Monument Hill, close to Oban, sorted the men from the boys. Carlsson was the only driver in the event to meet the target time, and victory was his. Even so, part way through the stage, co-driver Stuart Turner began to worry that they were being caught, because he thought he could see lights behind them – it later transpired that these were sparks from the sump shield as it skidded over the rocks!

With this, and with two further RAC rally victories to follow in the next two years, Saab's British legend was assured. Turner excelled as a co-driver,

They left it dirty, just for effect – though Erik Carlsson and Stuart Turner at least found time to don dinner jackets for the after-rally party of the 1960 RAC rally, which they had just won.

of course, particularly around the south of London on the final afternoon when the cars had to reach Brands Hatch in the Friday rush hour, but Erik's bravery on gravel surfaces made all the difference. It was not until years later that Erik admitted that he'd driven the event with cracked ribs – an injury sustained when he and Turner had spent time looking for potential special stages in Scotland (a practice that was, in any case, discouraged ...), and had a crash with a private car!

By the end of the season, therefore, 'works' Saabs had won no fewer than four major European rallies. The worth of the new model was succinctly summed up by that doyen of 'classic' rallying, John Gott, when he wrote his survey of International rallying for the season in *Autosport* magazine:

"The relative performances of the various marques can be most easily assessed from [the table] below ... This clearly shows up how good a rally car is the little Saab. Some may say that its wins were scored mainly under the specialised Scandinavian conditions, but a Saab was also second in the Polish, the Acropolis and the Tulip. The Saab owes its success to its wonderful road-holding and great strength, but there may be something in the practice of building a 'works' Saab from the beginning, rather than adapting a production car as do most of the British factories."

1961

Although no-one, surely, could have expected Saab to improve on the phenomenal 'first season' performance of 1960, the team put up yet another phenomenal performance in 1961. Not only did the 96 record three outright wins – one of them being in the incredibly demanding Acropolis rally of Greece – but there was also a second place in Poland, and third in the Tulip and the Midnight Sun, all of these in a car powered only by an 841cc engine of obsolescent two-stroke design.

Once again it was John Gott, the sage of the sport at this point in history, who summarised the season with this comment in his Annual Survey in *Autosport*:

"For the second year running the little Saab and the big Mercedes-Benz 220SE were the most consistently successful touring cars, nor were the Saab's successes, unlike those of the Mercedes, dependent on one brilliant crew. Both cars owed their success to magnificent road-holding and great sturdiness rather than to sheer power, and the engine is perhaps the weakest part of the Saab ..."

The season began, in fact, with huge controversy when the Monte Carlo rally organisers produced a format and a set of regulations which, on the one hand included flat-out special stages, but on the other hand imposed a handicapping system that favoured any heavy, under-powered, Group 1 car. In some ways that might have been to Saab's advantage, except that a further handicap reduced the competitiveness of two-stroke engines.

At a stroke these rules seemed to offer victory to a previously uncompetitive car, the French Panhard Tigre Saloon. For example, on the first of the stages (an 18.6 mile/30km dash south of Chambery), the Porsche 356, which, incidentally, went on to win the European Championship that year, would have had to beat a Panhard by 9 minutes 30 seconds to beat it on handicap. Ludicrous!

With Panhard assured of victory (in the end it took 1-2-3 but never again came close to winning a major event ...) Saab had to scratch around for respectability. If only because the 95 Estate car was heavier than the 96 Saloon, and because it had a four-speed gearbox in Group 1 form (the Saloon had a 3-speeder at this stage ...), Saab entered Erik Carlsson in one of those cars instead – the actual machine, they say, having already seen duty with the team as a service support vehicle.

If we ignore the handicap system that applied (and all serious rally pundits did just that), we see that this, the very first 'special stage' Monte, turned into a vigorous and straight fight between two front-wheel-drive cars – the Citroën DS19 of René Trautmann, and the Saab 95 Estate of Erik Carlsson. Trautmann was fastest overall, beating Carlsson by 3min 38 seconds over five long stages (the best of the Panhards was

For many years, Sweden's premier rally was the 'Midnight Sun,' held in June. This was the Skogh brothers in a two-stroke 96, on their way to winning the event in 1961.

With victory in the 1961 RAC rally of Great Britain already assured, Erik Carlsson swings the two-stroke 96 through the manoeuvring test on the sea front at Brighton at the end of the event.

no less than 15 minutes adrift), but the handicap allowed Erik to take fourth place, while Trautmann (even though he was French, in a French car) was relegated to obscurity, and nineteenth place.

For Saab, no more could possibly have been expected, but as far as all of rallying's real experts were concerned, the Swedish marque had delivered another outstanding performance. The team then had several months to settle back, let the 95 Estates be returned to more proper and more seemly use as service and support cars, and to re-prepare 96 Saloons for other European events.

The Tulip, as usual, linked a start and finish in Holland with Monte Carlo for a rest halt, and no fewer than fourteen speed tests or hill-climbs in the French and German mountains along the way. This time the handicapping system featured a 'class improvement' formula which eventually encouraged one Triumph Herald to be retired in favour of another, thus leaving a huge gap in that class, and handing that car outright victory.

Although Carl-Magnus Skogh led the event, on handicap, at half distance in Monte Carlo, Saab was fighting it out among its class rivals. However, since Skogh's car had beaten only two privately-entered examples, by a less than impressive margin, he had to settle for third place overall behind Mabbs' Herald and Hans Walter's Porsche 356 Carrera. And where was Erik Carlsson? Even before half distance, his 96 was seen on the end of a tow-rope, for an ignition distributor had failed, and put him out of the running.

Two weeks later, though, Erik, in another (freshly-prepared) 96, quite dominated the Greek Acropolis rally. This was the sort of event where driver courage, sheer motor car strength, and rugged reliability in hot and dusty weather combined to produce a result. As it transpired, the rough stages proved ideal for drivers with Scandinavian experience, which meant that this turned into a straight battle between Carlsson's tiny-engined Saab, and Gunnar Andersson's 1.8-litre, rear-drive Volvo. Although there was a performance handicap, this was not as extreme as that on the Monte Carlo, and, in fact, the Saab would still have won – narrowly – if all penalties had been calculated on a scratch-time basis.

By this time the Saab/front-wheel-drive combination was feared on any event where straight-line performance was not at issue, so when the best drivers and cars in Europe had to make a choice between racing along the swooping gravel stages of Sweden (in the Midnight Sun rally), or in the mountains of France, they chose the latter. The result was that in Sweden, Saab took first, third, fourth and fifth places, with Carl-Magnus Skogh winning yet another event for Saab.

Erik Carlsson took a car to Marseilles to contest the French rally, but he didn't start (his highly-tuned Group 3 engine failed). Accordingly, it was time to shrug, trek all the way back to Sweden, and prepare for the Polish rally early in August. Even going to Poland (though it was geographically closer to Sweden) was a mixed blessing, for many other 'works' teams boycotted the event which was dominated by East-West politics. In the end, Skogh took second place overall, beaten only (on performance, naturally) by the formidable Böhringer/Aaltonen combination in a big Mercedes-Benz 220SE. Aaltonen, too, won the 1000 Lakes, in a similar Mercedes, where Skogh struggled to take fourth.

Erik Carlsson was away practising for the Liège-Sofia-Liège Marathon, an event the Saab might be expected to survive, though only if it could match this club's sometimes insane target average speeds. As it happened, the schedules were so outrageously demanding (and being one minute late often meant instant exclusion), and conditions so rough and car-breaking, that only eight cars finished. Erik's Group 3 Saab consumed a piston, which overheated and melted, so the trip was not worthwhile.

The last event of the season was Britain's own RAC, which might just have been designed for Saab. Not only was this the first RAC to rely on many Forestry Commission special stages to sort out a result, stages which ideally suited the front-wheel-drive Saab, but Carlsson had won the event in 1960.

The Saab 96/Erik Carlsson combination won Britain's RAC rally three times in succession – 1960, 1961 and 1962 – thus cementing the car's reputation in the UK for many years to come. Here is Erik in the wilderness of Culbin forest, in Scotland, in 1961.

Erik Carlsson returned to Britain to win his second RAC rally in 1961. Now that many special stages had been included for the first time, Erik shows just how far ahead he was of all his opposition. This was Mallory Park circuit on the penultimate morning.

For 1961, Carlsson elected to take motoring journalist John Brown as his co-driver (Stuart Turner had moved on to higher things, having recently become Competitions Manager of BMC). The car was fitted with the four-speed transmission and, almost as expected, completely dominated the event. The Saab took many fastest times, such that at the end of the five day route, which embraced England, Scotland and Wales, it was well clear of Pat Moss's Austin-Healey 3000 and Peter Harper's Sunbeam Rapier.

Could anyone now stop the Saab/Carlsson or Saab/Skogh combinations in demanding going? It didn't look like it ...

1962

The new season started well for Saab, having entered both Erik Carlsson and Carl-Magnus Skogh for the Monte. After the unfair farrago of 1961 the handicapping system had been drastically changed, and though it still favoured small-engined cars the advantage was now slight. The weather was quite unseasonably mild, with very little snow, and there were only five long special stages (along with a final time trial around the Monaco GP circuit). As it was, Carlsson put in another sterling performance to win the event outright from Eugen Böhringer's big Mercedes-Benz 220SE – incidentally, with or without handicap it would have made no difference, for the little Saab was just five seconds quicker overall! Skogh finished fourth in the capacity class, and sixteenth overall.

While most of the professional European rallying 'circus' then had a big lay off before the Tulip rally (Holland – Monte Carlo – Holland by way of the usual French and German speed tests), Saab sent two cars – for Erik Carlsson, and for Pat Moss (who, at that time, was already engaged to be married to Erik) – to compete in the East African Safari rally. One reason for this entry was that Erik had 'won' it, as one of his prizes, in the 1961 RAC rally. Bo Swaner recalls that it would not have been possible for Saab to compete in the Safari without financial help from Sears, the large American mail order concern.

Although the baldly stated results show Pat finishing third (being a VW Beetle and a Peugeot 404), and Erik following up in sixth place – the 'works' cars took first and second in their capacity class too – this cannot convey just what an impression the raucous two-strokes (which, according to strictly-enforced Safari regulations, were running in absolutely standard, though carefully prepared, condition) made on the knowledgeable observers. If Pat's Saab had not hit an animal at one stage, she could have taken second place, and if Erik's car had not broken its rear suspension ... if, if, if. A European crew would not win the Safari, in fact, for another decade.

The Tulip rally itself, in which Saab entered Carlsson and Carl-Magnus Skogh, was held in May. Once again this was an event riddled with a handicap, and though there was no authorised practising of the tests it was amazing how many co-drivers had sheets of pace notes when their cars arrived on start lines (the author was one of them). As there were only 90 miles of speed tests, mostly uphill, where

Erik Carlsson's first of two Monte Carlo victories came in January 1962. His co-driver was Gunnar Haggbom.

Casino Square in Monte Carlo, with Erik Carlsson on his way to a serene victory in the 1962 Monte Carlo rally. He would win again in 1963.

Saab's 96s never managed to win the East African Safari, even though they were extremely strong, and suitable for the going. This was Erik Carlsson in the 1962 event, where he was 'robbed' of victory by excessive under-body damage.

Porsches and the formidable Austin-Healey 3000s were bound to shine, Saab was always in trouble. Carlsson's car was very narrowly beaten on scratch times by Pierre Gelé's DKW Junior, while Skogh crashed out before the end of the event. This, it seems, was one of the last times we would see him in International motorsport in a Saab.

The Acropolis, which followed at the end of the month, set a totally different challenge, as usual a combination of rough roads, difficult special stages, dust and high temperatures. Carlsson and Skogh started (Skogh's car being fitted with the brand-new front-wheel disc brakes – these not yet having been homologated – that would follow in November 1962 – but being authorised by these particular regulations), but neither could quite keep up with the large, but deceptively fleet, Mercedes-Benz of Eugen Böhringer. After four days of Mediterranean torment, Skogh had retired when his disc brake installation had given trouble, while Carlsson was just, and only just, slower than the big Mercedes, and had to settle for second place. Second, a good result? Not to Erik, to whom winning was everything, and second was the first of the losers ...

By this time the team was learning how to build the still-to-be-homologated triple-carb Saab Sport, so there never seemed to be any older cars, or time, to spare. Short of ready-prepared rally cars, maybe, at that moment, Saab then gave the French Alpine a miss (it was too fast, with too much tarmac to attract Saab ...) but then made a big effort in its 'home' event, the Rally of the Midnight Sun. This was more like it – sweeping special stages, practice allowed, and a good deal of local support – so much was expected of the 'works' cars. If only the Saabs had a bit more performance it might have been enough, for in the end all of Erik Carlsson's heroics could not defeat the sheer straight-line performance of Bengt Soderstrom's BMC Mini-Cooper and Harry Bengtsson's Porsche.

Would there be better fortune on the Polish, which followed in August? Unhappily not, for this was the first occasion for some time in which Carlsson lived up to his old På Taket ('on the roof') reputation, by rolling his 96 into retirement. Normally, the egg-shaped Saab could be rolled back on to its wheels, but not this time ...

Saab's showing at the Finnish 1000 Lakes was more satisfactory, however, with Carlsson taking a sturdy third place overall, and a deceptively frail-looking young man called Simo Lampinen finishing fifth. Erik would undoubtedly have finished higher if Pauli Toivonen's front-wheel-drive Citroën DS19 had not put up such a stunning performance to take the victory.

The Saab's limitations were now beginning to show, but for the moment nothing could be done. On the Liège-Sofia-Liège marathon which followed, it didn't help that Carlsson's car sheared a rear shock absorber (the same thing had happened on the Safari, also in very rough conditions). Would it even be worth going to Germany in September? Not, as it turned out, for Carlsson's Saab, which suffered from persistent baulking from slower DKWs (of whom it was suggested that some of their slow driving was 'voluntary' ...), while Mercedes-Benz applied pressure to other private owners to make sure that Böhringer's showing was improved. Through no fault of his own, Carlsson's bid for the European Rally Championship was faltering.

Even so, Saab sent Carlsson to compete in the Geneva, another of those events that concentrated on familiar stages and speed tests in the French Alps, and which applied a much-derided performance-improvement handicap to theoretically give every car a chance. Unhappily, this didn't do Saab any favours, especially when it was clear that outright acceleration, uphill, was going to make all the difference. After a great deal of fruitless high-speed motoring, which regularly saw the 841cc-engined Saab in the top five, the gallant Saab finished second overall to Hans Walter's ultra-fast 2-litre Porsche 356 Carrera.

At the end of the season, however, Saab then sent just one 96 to Britain for the RAC rally, where Erik Carlsson was looking for his hat-trick of victories. On this occasion his co-driver was a young David Stone (who would soon team up with Vic Elford), and the car was in familiar specification. Starting from No. 4, and quite dominating

A 'works' Saab 96, 'yumping' a bridge in the early 1960s, in the British RAC rally. These were the days before safety provisions were paramount ...

Erik Carlsson won the British RAC rally three times in succession. In 1962, his co-driver was David Stone – and this special stage was run on a military proving ground.

the event from start to finish, Erik duly completed that hat-trick, winning by a considerable margin from Paddy Hopkirk's 'works' Austin-Healey 3000, and from his soon-to-be new wife, Pat Moss, who was third in another Big Healey. The stats tell their own story, for the Saab set fastest time on 18 of the 29 special stages, and was second fastest on eight others. On the longest stages the Saab's winning margins were sometimes enormous – 51 seconds in the 27 minute Wark forest stage, and 46 seconds in 26 minutes of Dovey, for instance. Böhringer's Mercedes-Benz crashed out of the event.

Although the European Championship title had now slipped away – Erik Carlsson finished second to Böhringer by a narrow margin – Saab could surely be happy with the results of the season. For 1963, however, there was rather ominous news, in that the 'works' BMC team would have its new 1.1-litre Mini-Cooper 1071S to play with – while the Swedes could not look forward to anything faster for some time to come.

283 is a famous competition number for all Saab 96 enthusiasts, as it was carried by Erik Carlsson's 96 when it won the Monte Carlo rally of 1963.

1963

Saab now began a race to keep up with the opposition – BMC and Ford in particular – whose new models were faster, more powerful, more specialised, and backed by bigger budgets. Although Saab still had cars that were as strong as anything fielded by the opposition, and Erik Carlsson was still one of the very best, and most successful, rally drivers in the world, the ever-realistic Swedes could see the day coming when this would not be enough.

Not that it seemed to show in January, when the Monte Carlo rally turned into one of the occasional winter nightmares which totally decimated the field. Only 96 of the 296 starters made it to the finish, and many of them were definitely 'walking wounded.' Not that this seemed to concern Erik Carlsson and his new co-driver Gunnar Palm at all, whose formidable talents were just right for fighting their way through deep and daunting snow and ice from the Stockholm start, and tackling the five long special stages which they had practised assiduously in advance. There was still a performance handicap to be accepted, of course, but in view of his 1962 victory with the same obstacles placed in his way, this did not worry him either.

Although the fastest car of all on the event (by more than four minutes) was Bo Ljungfeldt's 4.2-litre Ford Falcon (but he had road penalties), and Paul Toivonen's big Citroën was also 71 seconds faster, the magnificent Saab was third fastest on 'scratch,' and after the handicapping formula had been applied, Erik was a comfortable winner.

Fame and fortune, however, can soon disappear in motorsport, as Erik and Saab soon discovered. On the East African Safari, where the cars had performed so well in 1962, Saab had no luck at all. Although the 'works' car led the entire field by some hours, and for many hours, according to John Sprinzel's rally report:

" ... Not far from Mbulu, Carlsson suddenly slowed, and we hear that a collision with an ant-bear had pushed the anti-roll bar into the driveshaft universal ..."

Erik Carlsson and Gunnar Palm won the Monte Carlo rally of 1963, with a stunning performance in this two-stroke 96 model.

Having beaten the world's best on the snowy special stages of the 1963 Monte, Erik Carlsson enjoyed a quick sprint around the famous Grand Prix street circuit of Monte Carlo.

Erik Carlsson's 96 takes the start of the 1963 Safari, in a staged 'race' against star Kenyan runner Seraphino Antao ... the runner won over a 100-yard course!

Famous picture, famous car, famous occasion – the indomitable Carlsson on his way to victory in the 1963 Monte Carlo rally. The scene (where else!) was the famous Col du Turini in southern France.

The animal, otherwise described as an ant-eater or 'muhanga' inflicted damage where no ordinary East African road could do the same, for the Saab eventually lost a front wheel, stranding the crew in the bush, many miles from help.

Carlsson's car then retired from the Tulip rally with engine trouble, and from the Greek Acropolis after a crash, along with later blowing another engine on the French Alpine.

It was a different story on 'home gravel,' the Swedish Midnight Sun rally of mid-June. Only Bengt Jansson's 2-litre Porsche could stay ahead of Carlsson's 96 Sport – he won by 40 seconds – and no other car in the event could keep up. Saab horsepower might be limited to 80bhp, but Carlsson's bravery, it seemed, was limitless.

No more so, for sure, than in the Spa-Sofia-Liège Marathon which followed at the end of August, where rough roads, impossible target average speeds, and an almost complete lack of scheduled rest halts, made this the toughest of all European Championship events. Breakages, rather than lateness, were what eliminated most crews, yet the intrepid Saab/Carlsson/Palm combination kept going for four days and nights, ending up in second place overall, beaten only by the equally amazing Eugen Böhringer and his Mercedes-Benz 230SL. Only 20 cars – 16 per cent of the starters – made it back to the finish at Liège in Belgium. It was a phenomenal performance.

Finally, of course, came Saab's traditional attack on the British RAC rally. Although the company officially entered five cars – and showed an impressive line-up to prove this, which included Olle Dahl and Åke Andersson – the only truly serious entry came from Erik Carlsson. Could he turn the three successive victories into four? Or was the Saab finally running out of steam?

With more than 400 miles of special stages in a 2200 mile event, the route from Blackpool to Bournemouth was a real marathon, yet although the Carlsson/Saab was as formidable as usual, other Scandinavian driver/car combinations had finally caught up. Here was an early message to Saab – that Tom Trana and a 1.8-litre Volvo was now faster than the incredible Mr Carlsson, for the two-stroke engine had now reached its limits. Trana, and another Swede, Harry Kallstrom (VW1500S) finally beat Erik, who finished a gallant third (second-equal fastest on stages, but pushed down one place in a tie-break) and won his class.

1964

The big news for 1964 was not in the car's engineering, but in the driver line up. Having married Pat Moss in August 1963, Erik Carlsson then persuaded her to join him in the Saab 'works' team, this producing a really world-class line-up for the new season. Pat, one has to say, was both loyal and brave to make this move, as she was giving up 'works' 150bhp Ford Lotus-Cortinas (and had been driving 210bhp Austin-Healey 3000s as recently as 1962) to do this.

Saab's season then began as it was to go on, with the gallantly driven two-stroke Saabs trailing their characteristic haze of blue smoke, in a vain effort to keep up with the steadily increasing performance of more modern opposition. This was the year in which the Monte Carlo rally developed into a straight fight between Paddy Hopkirk's Mini-Cooper 1071S, and Bo Ljungfeldt's 4.7-litre Ford Falcon Sprint, with all their rivals, including Erik's Saab, and his wife Pat's Saab, being left well behind. Snow on the five special stages was in any case sparse, so the Saab was well out-gunned, though in the end third (Erik) and fifth (Pat) were fine performances.

Then came a rare excursion to Mediterranean Europe, where the same two Saabs which had competed in Monte Carlo returned to northern Italy, to take part in the Rallye dei Fiori (an event which would soon grow up into the San Remo). Although there was much competition from local Italian heroes, in Lancias, twisty and demanding stages, with much snow and other loose surfaces, proved to be ideal for the Saabs, and Erik won the event, with Pat (accompanied by Valerie Domleo) in second place.

Could Saab then win the Safari? Would it smash the seemingly unbreakable hoodoo that afflicted all European crews? Erik Carlsson, having led the event on previous

Pat Moss, in her Saab 96, on the circuit test on the Monaco F1 GP circuit, in the 1964 Monte Carlo rally. (Reproduced from the BP/Castrol Archive)

In the 1964 Monte Carlo rally, which proved a titanic battle against handicaps and the weather, Erik Carlsson's two-stroke 96 took third place overall. (Reproduced from the BP/Castrol Archive)

Pat Moss, carrying no. 56, took a fine fifth place in the 1964 Monte Carlo rally. Here she is on the Monaco GP circuit race at the end of the event. (Reproduced from the BP/Castrol Archive)

Erik Carlsson and Gunnar Palm in discussion with a Monaco official in the 1964 Monte Carlo rally. (Reproduced from the BP/Castrol Archive)

This is the unmistakeable 'location' shot – at the summit of the Col du Turini – on the 1964 Monte Carlo rally. It's all downhill to the end of the special stage from this point. (Reproduced from the BP/Castrol Archive)

When Pat Moss joined Saab for 1964, she helped make up a formidable team. Here, before the Rally of the Flowers in 1964 are (left-to-right) Pat Moss, Val Domleo, Erik Carlsson and Gunnar Palm.

occasions, thought it could be done, Pat Moss was determined to prove that if he could, then so could she – but it wasn't to be. This was the event in which Ford-UK seemed to spend what was equivalent to the Gross National Product of Kenya on winning the rally with its Cortina GTs. Local man Peter Hughes was both fast and secure in one of those cars, while Saab had misfortunes – Pat Moss' car suffering a badly damaged clutch at one point, and Erik finding his car stuck in the bush, on its belly, with all four wheels off the ground.

Nothing daunted, Erik and Gunnar Palm summoned help from the locals, rolled the car sideways out of trouble,

Although Saab never won the East African Safari, it came very close at times. In 1964, this two-stroke car finished second, just 11 minutes behind the outright winner.

Although the Carlsson/Saab 96 alliance was always the fast combination in the Safari, Erik never actually managed to win the event. This was 1964 – the 'Year of the Cortina.'

This famous sequence of pictures was taken on the 1964 Rally of the Midnight Sun when Erik Carlsson up-ended his two-stroke 96 on an airfield test. The car tipped over on to its side, Gunnar Palm leapt out of the right side door, and managed to wrestle the car back on to its wheels ...

A famous team; but not victorious. Pat Moss is partnered by Liz Nystrom, in a Saab 96 Sport, at the start of the French Alpine rally in 1964.

saw that there was no more than a slightly damaged roof, and carried on! Ford, incidentally, heard of this, and at the post-event prize-giving, decided to prove that a Cortina could also be rolled – on a dance floor. Precious fluids including battery acid spread around, and Ford was faced with a big bill to put matters right! In the end the Carlsson car took second place, 11 minutes behind the Cortina, while Pat finished ninth overall.

Although Erik Carlsson and co-driver, Gunnar Palm, enjoyed the French Alpine rally, their under-powered two-stroke 96 always struggled with uphill special stages. As Palm later quipped: "There was plenty of time to enjoy the scenery ..."

On reflection, Saab should not have troubled itself with the Tulip rally which followed, for it was run to the usual 'class improvement' performance handicap system, the 'works' 96s were running in the same class, and were therefore certain to negate each other's performance. And so it was. On the steep uphill speed tests that made up most of this event, Erik fought head-to-head with Pat, only beating her after she spun on one stage, and could not even win their capacity class, which was taken by K Pfenier's DKW F11.

Although there would be no more 'works' victories

Co-driver Gunnar Palm rated Erik Carlsson's hard-bitten drive to second place in the 1964 Spa-Sofia-Liège rally his finest-ever feat. Not even an 80bhp Saab could match the performance of Aaltonen's 210bhp Austin-Healey 3000! This was the early stage of the event, so the crew found time to wave at the photographer.

until 1966, there were many stirring performances to cheer up Saab enthusiasts. Pat Moss took third in the Acropolis, Åke Andersson managed fifth on the Swedish Midnight Sun event, which was encouraging – but the next sensation of the year came in France in June, when Erik Carlsson/Gunnar Palm took second place overall in the touring category of the French Alpine.

If that all-tarmac road race had been held on scratch timing, then the Saab would have had no chance, but as different test and road section target times were allowed for different engine sizes (and Appendix J groups) it allowed outstanding small cars to have a chance, too. In a high-summer/high-mountains event where Ford Lotus-Cortinas fought head-to-head against Mini-Cooper 1275Ss and Austin-Healey 3000s, Erik Carlsson's magnificent never-say-die performance in his 841cc Saab impressed everyone. Only seven cars ended up 'clean' on the road – one of them being the valiant Saab.

In the meantime, a young man called Simo Lampinen won the Finnish Rally of the 1000 Lakes outright in a privately-prepared 96. The sensational thing was not only that he did this without overt factory assistance, but that he was physically handicapped, with a serious limp: the after-effects of a childhood attack of polio. We would hear more of Simo in the future – for not only would he join the Triumph 'works' team for 1965, but he would then win world-class rallies in Saabs, and other makes of car, in a long and distinguished rallying career.

The last of Europe's great rallying 'road races' – Spa–Sofia-Liège – was then held in August, and produced one of the best performances the Carlsson/Saab combination ever put up. In this exhausting 96-hour event, which covered almost 3500 miles, the route was run off with no more than a single one-hour halt at Sofia, in Bulgaria. There were no milk-and-water class handicaps, so the combination of impossible time schedules, rough roads, speed, endurance, and sheer exhaustion meant that few managed to finish.

In what co-driver Gunnar Palm often describes as Erik's finest-ever drive ("he never stopped going absolutely flat out – and neither did the car"), the Saab ended up in a magnificent second place. The performance of this particular car (it was registered PA12526) was even better than usual for a 96, because the generously loose regulations that applied on this event allowed it to use many lightweight parts. Rauno Aaltonen's 210bhp Austin-Healey 3000 won, with a lateness penalty of 57 minutes, so Carlsson's achievement in losing only 85 minutes in a tiny-engined Saab was quite amazing. Not even Böhringer's Mercedes-Benz 230SL, nor Pat Moss could keep up with that. It was an utterly unbelievable performance.

By comparison, for the Geneva rally, a gentle race around the French mountains was almost relaxing, where Carlsson took advantage of yet another favourable class handicap to take third place behind a 4.7-litre Ford Falcon and a white-hot 'works' Triumph Spitfire, while Pat Moss followed him home in the class, seventh overall.

Which meant that the season's traditional closing event, the British RAC rally, was the only chance Saab still had to add more victories in 1964, but this opportunity disappeared in the Taliesin stage in Wales when Carlsson's 96 Sport took a wrong turning (a directional arrow was apparently obscured) and dropped him so far down the field that he could finish only seventh. Time, and progress, it seemed, were catching up with Saab, for Trana's Volvo, Makinen's Big Healey and Vic Elford's Ford Cortina GT were all faster than Pat Moss' 96 Sport, which nevertheless took fourth place.

1965

Although it was surely time for a big rethink of motorsport policy at Trollhättan, the rally team soon came to the conclusion that it could do little more than soldier on with the existing 96 Sport, for there was no more that could be done to make it any faster. It was already strong, already had an 80+bhp engine, but could do no better than that.

Amazingly, though, the 'works' cars continued to shine in events suited to their particular strengths. In Monte Carlo, for instance, blizzard-like conditions swept away most of the entry, but suited the Saabs, which combined winter-

The Monte Carlo rally of 1965 was held in blizzard-like conditions. Erik Carlsson's car succumbed to carburettor icing problems, but Pat Moss (seen here) finished a remarkable third overall.

proven chassis, the best in studded tyres, and the unearthly skills of the drivers (all of which explains why Pat Moss took a remarkable third place overall). All the headlines were full of Timo Makinen's astonishing victory in a Mini-Cooper S, of course, and Eugen Böhringer's chase in a Porsche 904 (which was really a racing sports car!), but Pat's Saab was nevertheless the first 'ordinary' car to make it to the finish. Erik's car dropped out with carburettor icing problems.

The so-called Midnight Sun rally of Sweden was now run in March (when daylight hours were very few), but the snow and ice suited the Saabs. Åke Andersson's 96 Sport took second place overall to Tom Trana's Volvo. Much more publicity (but of what kind?) was then generated when Erik Carlsson started the Safari rally, his illustrious co-driver none other than Stirling Moss.

It was typical of Stirling that he took matters very seriously, and all might have been well if the car's own navigational device (a Swedish Halda Tripmaster) had not packed up, rendering all the crew's notes and practice useless, so retirement was inevitable.

The Tulip rally was a real milk-and-water exercise, where uphill on speed tests, and another of those frustrating

When the going gets tough, the tough get going – Erik Carlsson and this two-stroke car finished second in the 1965 Acropolis rally, close behind a much bigger and faster Volvo.

handicapping systems, meant that Saab was always struggling. Private entrants Hans Lund and Olle Dahl, however, plugged on, won their class, and ended up winning the entire Touring category.

The Acropolis was a much more serious affair, with no handicap to get in the way, with rough roads and high target averages to be met – and with real competition. From start to finish, both Erik Carlsson and Åke Andersson's 'works' cars were in the fight for the lead, and when only fifteen cars actually reached the end, it all came down to a sprint up the Parnis hill-climb, and a half-hour circuit race at Tatoi airfield. The result, agonisingly close, was that Skogh's Volvo 122 Amazon narrowly defeated Carlsson, while Åke Andersson then took fourth place.

When the factory then ignored the Czech and French Alpine rallies, it was beginning to look like a difficult year for Saab, so a hearty third place (for Erik Carlsson) and fifth (for Pat Moss) in the Polish was a real boost. There was, however, little success in the Rally of 1000 Lakes, though Simo Lampinen once again shone, taking fourth place in his 96 Sport.

As ever, the climax of the season came in Britain, where the RAC rally attracted a huge entry, lots of stages and – as it happened on this occasion – mountains of snow and ice. London to London by way of Perth in Scotland included no fewer than 57 special stages. Normally speaking (if anything can be 'normal' in this type of motorsport), conditions should have been ideal for Saab, but as things turned out there was a five-day long running battle between Timo Makinen's Austin-Healey 3000 and Rauno Aaltonen's BMC Mini-Cooper S.

There were 'works' 96 Sports for three-times winner Erik Carlsson, Pat Moss (both in Group 3 cars, modified beyond homologated specification), Ove Andersson and Åke Andersson, along with several other well-supported private entries. Erik's, by the way, had already competed in the 1964 Spa-Sofia-Liège (and had the old-style nose shape), but had been thoroughly rebuilt since then. At half-distance, Makinen led Aaltonen, but Erik Carlsson was third, and

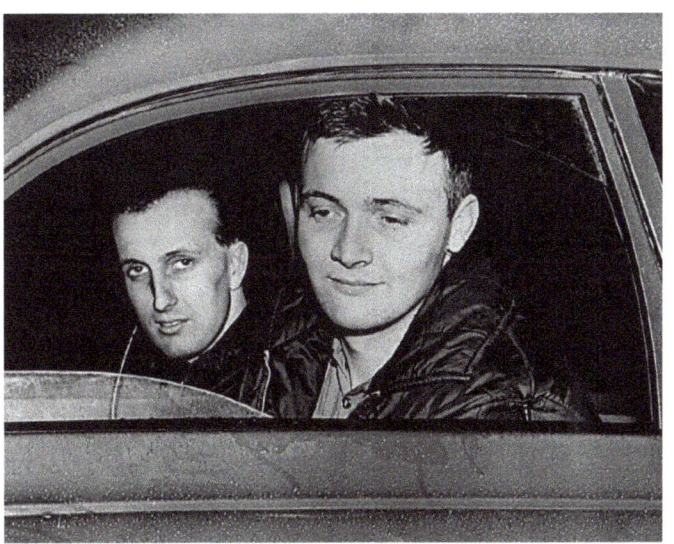

Ove Andersson looks slightly the worse for wear in this end-of-rally picture. His co-driver is Torsten Aman.

looking strong, with private-entry Jerry Larsson's car in fifth place.

Then came the carnage of the final two days, including stages in the Lake District and in Wales, where many cars dropped out, and where snow threatened to bring the rally to a grinding halt on several occasions. No matter how hard the two-stroke Saabs tried, they could not catch the two leaders, the result being that Jerry Larsson just caught and overtook Erik Carlsson to take third place. Pat Moss finished tenth, and second in her capacity class, behind husband Erik.

It was the end of an eventful season, in which, to be honest, Saab had struggled to stay competitive, but in which it proved yet again that strength, reliability and super-star drivers can make up for a lot.

1966

Was it now all over for the Saab 96? The factory, of course, did not think so, but the opinion of many media pundits is

Åke Andersson (right) and Sven Olof Svedberg were Saab team members in the mid-1960s. This posed shot was taken before the 1966 Swedish KAK rally, where the two-stroke 96 recorded its last, famous, victory.

Åke Andersson recorded the last major victory for the two-stroke 96, in the Swedish rally of 1966. Thereafter, the team began to work on four-stroke V4 models.

On the Safari – this was 1966 – one way to check if a flooded road was passable was to send the co-driver ahead to run through the flood. Torsten Aman doing what he was told ...

summed up by this comment, from John Davenport, in his end-of-1966 survey in *Autosport*:

"The Swedish factory of Saab, once champions of Europe with the small factory, the small car and the big driver, are now finding that strength and roadholding are not enough when the emphasis of rallying is swinging towards more special stages ..."

Saab and its bosses were not stupid, so spent the year picking and choosing, entering events for which the cars were still competitive, contesting others in odd cars (Sonetts on the French Alpine, for instance!), and generally waiting for the arrival of the V4, which would be revealed to the public in July.

Wisely ignoring the Monte Carlo rally (which, as it happened, descended to a chauvinistic farce over headlamp legalities, and disqualification for the 'works' Mini-Coopers), Saab prepared cars for ice-bound Sweden, which was obviously wise. The results show Saab taking 1-2-4-6, which was emphatic, to say the least. Åke Andersson only just made it to the end to win, for his car's transmission was leaking prodigious amounts of oil, but Simo Lampinen was always ready to take over if the car had failed. As for Erik Carlsson? The highly-tuned two-stroke engine failed – one might say 'again,' for these power units were well and truly at their limits.

A full-blooded attack on the East African Safari (it was now traditional, it seemed, for Saab to do this, even though the cars were not sold in numbers in East Africa), but it came to nothing when Erik Carlsson's engine (Group 1 – 'showroom standard' – or not) blew up, while Pat Moss' car had to be withdrawn when the suspension cracked.

Another two-stroke engine let go on the Tulip (the car used by Erik was very old – still having the old, 1964-style, front-end), while Pat Moss made a big joke of the entire proceedings by driving a 4.5-litre Plymouth Barracuda Coupé, for which Saab had the Swedish concession. Although she won the Coupe des Dames, the monstrous car from Detroit was well down the lists. Usually, a 'works' Saab would carry a window sticker telling the world that it was 'Made in Trollhättan by Trolls' – but for this car, the placard was 'Made in Detroit by Idiots.'

Saab's entry in the Acropolis rally was also disastrous – Carlsson could not start – for he was still carrying a back injury from the Safari – Pat Moss' engine blew up (this was getting ridiculous), and third-man Carl Orrenius found it difficult to stay on terms with other makes of car. In the end, he could only take fifth place which, by Saab's own standards, was a failure. Åke Andersson and Pat Moss both borrowed a 'works' car to compete in the British Gulf London rally, which was a real special stage marathon. The result was a triumph, with Åke winning, Pat second, and all the rest trailing.

Pat Moss took fifth in the Rally Vltava (Czechoslovakia), but there was no success in Germany or in Poland. Even in the 1000 Lakes (home territory for the fleet of Saab owners), the 96 was thoroughly blown away by the performance of the 'works' Mini-Cooper S, and Volvo types. Pat and Erik both tried out 90bhp/940cc-engined Sonett Coupés, in prototype form, in the French Alpine, but both cars retired with engine failure, and Pat's 96 Sport was a long way off the pace in the Three Cities (Munich-Vienna-Budapest) event.

Before the end of the year, there was only one possible chance that the Saabs might succeed, that being on our own British RAC rally. In 1966, though, this proved to be a real battle of attrition, where many fancied cars dropped out, and many headlines were made by F1 World Champion Jim Clark, who competed in (and crashed) a 'works' Lotus-Cortina.

Three cars – driven by Erik Carlsson, Pat Moss and Åke Andersson – took the start, which promised London-to-London by way of Wales, the Lake District, Aviemore (a night halt), Yorkshire and back to London, with no fewer than 68 special stages. In theory, this was ideal for Saab, but it all went wrong when the cars found themselves thoroughly outpaced. Andersson's car seized its engine before half distance, Carlsson's engine followed suit in Northumberland, while Pat Moss finished ninth, a long way off the pace, but still winning the Ladies' Award.

All in all, for Saab it had been an extremely disappointing season.

1967

OK, deep breath time. Saab simply had to wash its hands of the old two-stroke engine, and hope that it would be more competitive with a four-stroke power unit – even if that was the very simple, basically-engineered, 1.5-litre V4 from Ford-Germany. Nor was that all. Team leader, Erik Carlsson, was suffering more and more discomfort from a back injury, which had been inflicted on him by the incessant pounding of Saab rally cars.

For Saab, this was a difficult year. In sixteen European Championship rallies, there was only a single victory (for Erik Carlsson in the Czechoslovakian event), three second places (two of them to Simo Lampinen), and a third for Pat Moss in Czechoslovakia. Elsewhere it was still a real struggle.

The new V4 model had been homologated on 1 November 1966, so the team had enough time to prepare for the new season. The factory ignored the Monte Carlo rally, in favour of its own Swedish event, where a fleet of newly-built V4s started their first European Championship event. Not that everything went well, for Orrenius' car broke its distributor, Carlsson's car a cylinder head gasket, and Åke Andersson's car its transmission. Simo Lampinen's car, though, took second place, behind a Lotus-Cortina and ahead of a Mini-Cooper S.

To quote rally reporter John Davenport: "Before the start, Saab were firm favourites; their new V4 is much quicker than the two-stroke cars they were using last year ..." – which was encouraging.

Not that this helped on the Flowers/San Remo, where Pat Moss' V4 was refused the start because she did not have homologation papers with her. Now, if this had been an Italian car, in Italy ...

With no entry in Lyon-Charbonnières, and (surprising, this) none in the Safari, the team next attacked the Tulip, which was its usual steep hill-climbs/class-formula-handicap event. There was only one car, for Pat Moss in a V4 but after it broke a driveshaft on the start line of the very first test, that was effectively game over, for it took mechanics more than 30 minutes to repair the damage. Amazing, Lasse Jonsson's privately-entered V4 took second place in the Austrian Alpine (there were no 'works' cars on parade), and because no team cars started the Acropolis or the Geneva either, Saab's hopes were pinned on the non-Championship

These were the conditions for which the original Saab was designed – gravel roads (often snow-covered as here), cold weather and remote conditions. This was the Swedish rally of 1967.

Pat Moss thoroughly enjoyed her four years with the Saab rally team. Here she is, winning the Ladies' Prize on the Tulip rally of 1967 in one of the early V4s.

Erik Carlsson's final outright victory for Saab came in Czechoslovakia in 1967. It was the end of a glittering career.

Gulf London, which was a colossal three days and nights marathon with more stages (and less rest!) than any other British rally of the period.

Erik and Pat had Group 5 V4s, with twin-carburettor engines and lightweight bodywork, while Orrenius, Lampinen and Hakan Lindberg had normal Group 2 cars. During this gruelling event, each and every car suffered from transmission problems, and only two of them – Orrenius (4th) and Lampinen (5th) finished well up the leader board, Simo's car slowing perceptibly towards the close to keep the seemingly fragile transmission in one piece.

A visit to Czechoslovakia, on the other hand, produced Saab's only major victory of the year – and was also an excellent, and fitting, swan song to Erik Carlsson's glittering final year at European level. Two 96s started – for Erik and Pat – and both cars duly finished first and second on scratch times. It was only the organisers' complex engine size/handicapping system that then allowed Sobieslaw Zasada's so-called 'Group 1' Porsche 912 to move up to second place, splitting the husband-and-wife Saab team.

Although Saab could not possibly have forecast it, this was a suitable high point for Erik to bow out, for there would be no more important outright victories to celebrate until the very end of 1968, and then nothing more until 1971, when the young Stig Blomqvist had become a fully-matured Swedish superstar.

There were no factory entries in the Danube and Polish rallies that followed, for Saab was concentrating on the Finnish Rally of 1000 Lakes run in August. The early stages of what was now becoming known as the 'Finnish GP' saw Porsche 911s battling with fuel-injected 'works' Lotus-Cortinas, and Mini-Cooper S types, so the Saab V4s were somewhat breathless. Even so, Simo Lampinen set a number of fastest stage times in his V4, the Porsches and Fords eventually eliminated themselves (mainly in accidents), and it became a straightforward, but very tight, battle between Timo Makinen's 'works' Mini-Cooper S, and Lampinen's Saab. The V4 led until just four stages from home, after which Makinen beat Simo three times – by three seconds, one second and six seconds – which meant that the Saab lost out by a mere eight seconds, which made it one of the tightest European Championship finishes yet seen.

Saab then ignored the French Alpine (which was wise, as the 1967 event was a real high-altitude/tarmac road race), and the Spanish, for it had its sights on the most prestigious of all late-season events, the British RAC rally. This event, as we all now know, was to have included 69 special stages, and allowed prototype cars to compete, but was cancelled just 12 hours before the start because a nationwide outbreak of bovine foot-and-mouth disease meant that many roads were banned to vehicular traffic, and the route would have been cut to ribbons.

For Saab, the sporting tragedy was that it had a formidable team of V4s lined up – Erik Carlsson, Pat Moss, Simo Lampinen, Tom Trana and Carl Orrenius, with Erik, Trana and Orrenius all due to use 140bhp/1737cc prototype machines. Pat Moss was due to make her final appearance for Saab, as she had announced that she would be driving for Lancia in the future.

Cancellation was a bitter blow to everyone, not least the foreign entrants whose pockets suffered when the British currency was devalued during the weekend. For Saab, the only light relief came when an impromptu special stage was organised at Camberley at very short notice, so that rally cars could perform in front of TV cameras. This made for very good publicity for Saab, who sent Erik and Pat along to compete. To quote rally reporter John Davenport:

"The stage was only about four miles long, but was terribly rough, and on both timed runs Erik Carlsson showed the Saab and his own inimitable driving technique to the best advantage, by making fastest time and collecting first prize. However, he did suffer clutch failure during his second run, so his rally, if it had been held, might have been fast but short ..."

1968

With Erik Carlsson now retired, and with Pat Moss driving for Lancia, it was all change for what had suddenly become a more modest Saab team. By the end of the year there had

When Erik Carlsson retired, Bo Hellberg was very happy to sign up Tom Trana to join the works team in the late 1960s. Left-to-right: Tom Trana, Bo Hellberg, and co-driver Torsten Aman.

Night-time action, in a Saab V4, in the Swedish rally of the late 1960s. Note the 'Made in Trollhättan by Trolls' sticker in the side window.

Even the Saab V4 suffered from understeer at times – this is Tom Trana, well sideways, on the Karstad trotting track in the 1968 Swedish KAK rally (he finished second overall).

Private owners tackling the lack of grip on sheet ice in the Swedish rally – one V4 is well sideways with all wheels pointing ahead, while the other has terminal understeer.

Jerry Larsson and Torsten Palm, using this works-supported V4, took seventh place in the Swedish KAK rally of 1968.

been only one victory, and four other podium finishes. Simo Lampinen was the star driver and, as usual, Saab's battle was against more powerful and more specialised cars.

The season started in snow-bound Sweden, where Lampinen, Orrenius, Trana and Hakan Lindberg had to face up to 'works' Lotus-Cortinas and the formidable Swedish-prepared Porsche 911Ts. In the end it was 'no contest,' with Waldegård's 911T defeating Trana's and Lindberg's Saabs. Lampinen's V4 suffered a burned-through feeder pipe to the oil cooler, while Orrenius' car hit a fully-grown moose, a collision which killed both animal and car.

Two cars – for Trana and Orrenius – started the Monte, but Trana was way down in sixteenth place and Orrenius nowhere. After months back in Sweden, Trana and Orrenius then re-appeared on the Austrian Alpine, in Group 2 cars for which 115bhp was claimed, but Trana could finish no higher than ninth (spending more than eight minutes in a ditch didn't help).

Amazingly, Saab then ignored the Acropolis, a rough and tough event which should have been good for Saab, but instead sent three Group 6 cars with 1.7-litre engines, and about 120bhp – Lampinen, Orrenius and Jerry Larsson – to tackle the non-Championship Scottish. Using a much-modified Group 6 car, Orrenius actually led the event at half-distance (where Roger Clark had been expected to dominate in his new Escort Twin-Cam). The Saab then broke a driveshaft soon after the start, which left Clark miles in the lead, and at the close Simo Lampinen achieved fourth place, salvaging some honour for Saab.

The same cars, refurbished, then stayed in the UK to compete in the Gulf London rally, which turned out to be the toughest of all special stage rallies ever held in the country (three days and nights, 78 special stages, and only one hour for food and a shower at half-distance). Endurance – car and crew – rather than sheer performance would decide the winner here – Åke Andersson in a Swedish-prepared Porsche 911L. In the end just one V4, for Carl Orrenius, made it to the end, in a very creditable third place overall.

Soon after this, Saab sent two cars to Czechoslovakia,

Simo Lampinen (right) and John Davenport drove the winning Saab V4 in the RAC rally of 1968.

but once again their limited performance was a handicap. Simo Lampinen's V4 took a gallant second place, with Hakan Lindberg fourth, but this was against projectiles

Simo Lampinen and his English co-driver John Davenport used this V4 to win the 1968 RAC rally outright.

like Jean Vinatier's Alpine-Renault (which won) and Gilbert Staepelaere's Ford Escort Twin-Cam, which finished third.

Hopes, however, were higher for a good result in the Finnish 1000 Lakes – home territory for Simo Lampinen, who had already won the event twice in Finnish-prepared two-stroke 96s – but no-one could have forecast just how astonishing would be the performance of a youthful Hannu Mikkola in his first outing in an Escort Twin-Cam. Not even Lampinen could keep up with this meteoric car, so in the end his V4 had to settle for second place.

The team's only outright victory came at the very end of the season, when Simo Lampinen won the British RAC rally – though one must not read too much into this. Because the event took place just one week ahead of the start of the much-hyped London-Sydney Marathon, there were no 'works' entries in the RAC from Ford or BMC/British Leyland, so Saab's main opposition came from Lancia (no fewer than six Fulvia HFs) and three Porsche 911s. As ever, the event was to cover the length and breadth of Britain, with no fewer than 87 special stages – in other words, a real test for the toughest and most robust cars. Saab sent three V4s for Lampinen, Trana and Orrenius, all of them running in Group 2 form: limited-slip differentials – which gave trouble – were being tried for the first time.

Right from the start, Simo Lampinen and Carl Orrenius began battling for the lead, their principal opposition coming from Timo Makinen in a privately-entered Ford Escort Twin-Cam, and Vic Elford's Porsche, but Tom Trana's V4 retired with a broken limited-slip differential. Although there was mechanical carnage in the second part of the event – Elford, Makinen, and many other fancied runners all dropped out, and only 35 cars made it to the finish in London – the two leading Saabs kept going, looking more and more comfortable as time went on.

When all the results were counted, Lampinen was seen to have beaten Orrenius by more than 15 minutes, with the next surviving car (Jimmy Bullough's privately-built Ford Escort Twin-Cam) another twenty minutes away. It was a satisfying end to a very frustrating season.

1969

What followed was a very quiet, unspectacular, year. Now that Lancia's 1.6-litre Fulvia had been homologated, the Ford Escort Twin-Cam had become more reliable, and Porsche could always be guaranteed to be competitive (if it could be bothered to turn up for events), Saab's V4 was, it seemed, becoming an also ran. Although the driving strength was as high as ever – Simo Lampinen and Carl Orrenius were the leading personalities – between them they could only

For a time this was an almost unbeatable combination in wintry conditions – Simo Lampinen at the wheel of a V4.

manage three second places (Sweden, 1000 Lakes and the RAC) and one third place (Austrian Alpine). It didn't help that Saab spent a great deal of money sending Simo Lampinen out to tackle the Safari, where his car retired with a seized engine after only 50 miles.

But all was not lost. Even though there would now be no major victories until 1971, the team would bounce back in 1970 to take fourth in the World Championship for Makes, and a new Superstar driver – Stig Blomqvist – would brighten up its chances.

In Sweden, in the late 1960s, rallying was dominated by front-wheel-drive Saabs. This particular car shows off the interim nose style, with the elongated centre grille, but still with circular headlamps. More changes were on the way ...

So, to the highlights. In Sweden, amid the snow and ice that had always favoured Saab, there were four 'works' Group 2 cars, all now of the rectangular headlamp variety, all were competitive, the main battle being with Porsche and Lancia. In the end, Lampinen made mincemeat of the Lancias, but had no answer to the sheer horsepower and

Although this looks like a standard V4, in fact it was a much-lightened, more specialised, Group 6 machine. Simo Lampinen used it to win the 1969 Scottish rally.

To the winners, the spoils. Simo Lampinen (right) and Arne Hertz, with the trophies they won for victory in the 1969 Scottish rally (with two of the Shell model girls).

Saab mechanics from Trollhättan get ready to support their team cars on a major event. Finding space for all the wheels and tyres was always a problem.

traction of Bjorn Waldegård's Porsche and took second place, though ominously for the future, his V4 needed a complete transmission change at one point to keep it going.

Another fine performance came in the Austrian Alpine in May, which was a short but competitive event. No-one could catch Mikkola's Escort, or Kallstrom's Lancia Fulvia, but the three works V4s took third/fourth/fifth for Orrenius, Lampinen and Lars Jonsson.

Three weeks later, after ignoring the rough, tough and demanding Acropolis, Saab sent a Group 6 car to compete in the Scottish, this car retaining an homologated engine, but a much lightened (by 350lb/160kg) body shell. Although Roger Clark's Escort was hot favourite to win the event, his car broke down, so Simo took a fine victory, which cheered up the popular Swedish team considerably. Simo then managed only fourth in the Czech (his V4 was out-gunned),

Two famous faces – Erik Carlsson (right) and film superstar Steve McQueen – with the Saab V4 that Saab had prepared for the Baja 1000 race of 1969.

They don't come much tougher than this – Saab's V4, as specially prepared for Erik Carlsson to race in the 1969 Baja 1000. Note the line of the exhaust pipe, which was routed up the side of the windscreen pillar, then back towards the tail.

and second overall in the 1000 Lakes, while Timo Makinen (legendary in other makes of cars) took fourth place in a one-off drive in a Saab 96.

Saab then retreated to Trollhättan, and prepared for a serious assault on the RAC rally, where the V4 would, at the very least, be competitive. With that in mind, four factory cars (for Lampinen, Trana, Orrenius and Lindberg) were joined by two supported private owners, Stig Blomqvist and Per Eklund, all of them running in well-proven Group 2 guise. Yet with 73 special stages to come, how many would survive?

Few of them did. Lampinen's car blew both cylinder head gaskets on the first day, Blomqvist's, Eklund's and Lindberg's cars all went off the road, while the others struggled to keep up with the Escorts, Porsches and the Lancias. Orrenius and Trana were third and fourth at half distance, but at the end of the event, it was Orrenius who came closest to victory, taking second place to Kallstrom's Lancia Fulvia 1600HF, more than four minutes behind him.

Amazingly, before the end of the season, Saab-USA persuaded the factory to build a special V4 to compete in the Baja 1000 race, which covered about 1000 miles, was expected to take no more than 20 or 21 hours, and ran through the wildest territory in Mexico. Erik Carlsson was persuaded to come out of retirement for this event; he took along his regular co-driver Torsten Aman, and enjoyed the use of a brand-new, super-rugged V4. Ingvar Lindqvist, a Saab dealer from Los Angeles, drove a sister car.

This was an event that the indomitable Carlsson so nearly won. Although he had to face up to monstrously powerful American specials, he was always on the pace, until his

In 1969 Erik Carlsson came out of retirement to compete in the Baja 1000 race, a harum-scarum, flat-out, days-long dash held in Mexico. In spite of trouble with broken driveshafts, he finished third in the Production Car category.

117bhp-powered car broke a transmission driveshaft, this breakdown being repeated some hours later. At the end, which came 27 hours 32 minutes after the start, he finished third in the Production Car category – with the experienced Lindqvist the winner.

1970

Because the International Rally Championship was reduced to only seven events, this became yet another quiet year for the V4, even though fuel injection and twin Weber carburettors were now being tried out on the Group 2 engines. Because

the most glamorous teams and competitors were all away on the *Daily Mirror* London-Mexico World Cup Rally in April and May, or were preparing for it for weeks beforehand.

There was little activity in the second half of the season, for Saab ignored the 1000 Lakes (not a Championship qualifier), though to make up for this, it entered no fewer than four fuel-injected V4s for the British RAC rally. Blomqvist, Lindberg, Trana and Orrenius all turned up. It was the sort of event which should have suited Saab, and indeed for a time the injected V4s were absolutely on the pace. Unhappily, Stig Blomqvist then took a wrong turning in a stage and

A good joke! Team driver Tom Trana posing with the 'winter survival kit' which Saab recommended should be carried in the depths of the Scandinavian winter.

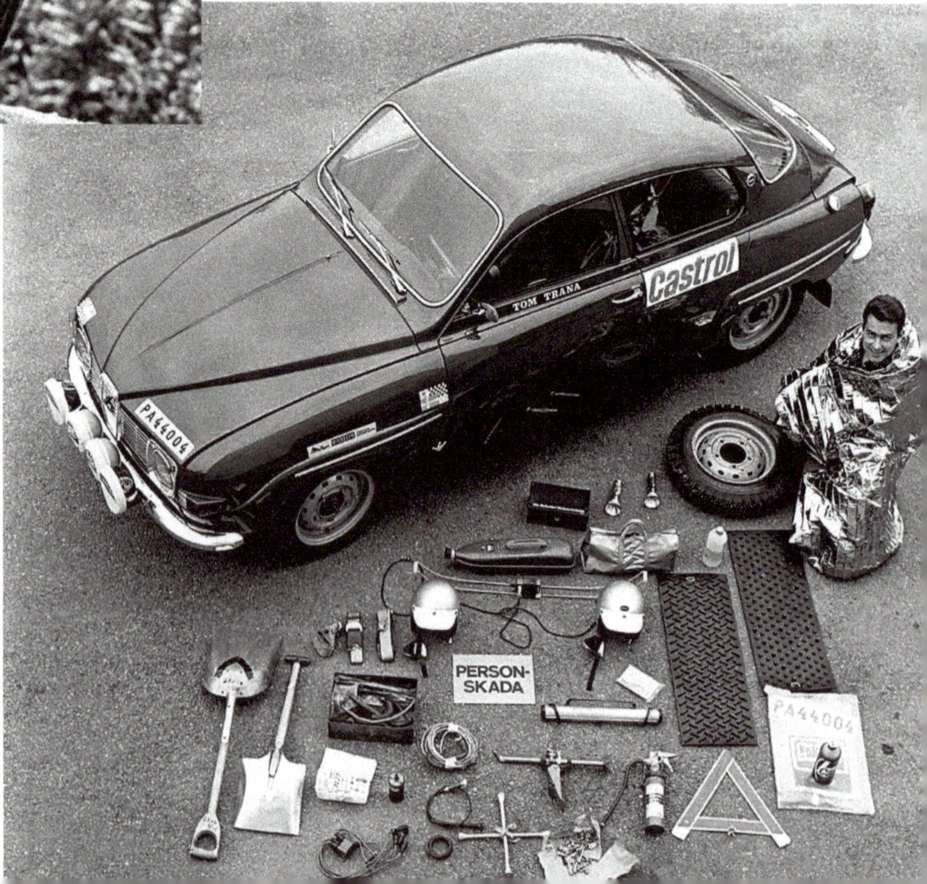

Saabs always jumped very well – this being John Unnerud's car in Norway in 1970.

Simo Lampinen had left the team (he was tempted away by a big-money contract from Lancia), Hakan Lindberg, Carl Orrenius, Tom Trana, Stig Blomqvist and Per Eklund shared the 'works' team's driving duties.

Stig Blomqvist took second place in the snow-bound Swedish (nothing could keep up with Waldegård's Porsche 911s at this point in history), Tom Trana took fourth in San Remo, Hakan Lindberg was second in the Austrian Alpine (beaten by Waldegård's Porsche 911, of course) – but this was a rather anonymous start to a season, as lost a lot of time, while the other cars all dropped out with transmission bothers – broken driveshaft, sheared gearbox pinion, and unspecified gearbox failure.

At the end of the season, therefore, Saab was fourth in the Championship, well beaten by Porsche, Alpine-Renault and Lancia, all of which were using very specialised cars, and carrying a great deal of special homologated equipment.

Determined to improve on its performance in the California-based Baja 1000, two new V4s – driven by Erik Carlsson and Pat Moss – were entered for the 1970 event. Unhappily, the team was no luckier than it had been in 1969, with Erik finishing fifth in his category.

1971

There followed a very strange season for the popular Swedish team, for they scored World Championship points on only two events – but both were outright victories. After looking at the eight-event calendar, it might have been easy to pick the Swedish and British RAC (both snowy 'winter' events) as those most likely to favour Saab – and this is precisely what happened. Outright victory in the non-Championship 1000 Lakes, in the Finnish Hankiralli, and in Norway all helped in this Scandinavian-orientated programme.

Two 'works' V4s started the Swedish – a 1815cc-engined car for Stig Blomqvist, and a 1740cc-engined car for Tom Trana. Ford Escorts, Porsche 911s and Lancias represented the main opposition, but right from the start it was Blomqvist's Saab V4 that took the lead, held it, and increased it. By the end, Blomqvist had eased out his lead to a comfortable five minutes, though Waldegård's Porsche 911S would have been closer than fourth if he had not picked up penalties for an open-road speeding offence. Stig set six fastest stage times out of the 39 which were scheduled, though Tom Trana was a long way back, in tenth place.

Stig Blomqvist always made up for the V4's lack of power by getting it more sideways than anyone else! This was the Finnish Hankiralli of 1977.

Two of Saab's regular rally heroes were Simo Lampinen (left) and Torsten Palm, here ready to tackle the 1967 Swedish rally.

Happy people on home ground, this being Sweden in 1972, with Bo Swaner (far left) and Bo Hellberg (far right) congratulating Arne Hertz and Stig Blomqvist on yet another International victory.

Where else but Sweden in 1971, when Stig Blomqvist was on his way to a comfortable victory in the KAK Swedish rally in his Group 2, 1815cc-engined V4.

In 1971 Saab tackled the Safari with material and financial help from Sears Roebuck of the USA. Here, Tom Trana is showing the big difference between small 'standard size' V4 rally tyres, and the big covers provided by Sears.

Having also won the Arctic rally Stig, bit between his teeth, then won the Finnish Snow (Hankiralli) as well, demonstrating that the 1740cc-engined V4 was a formidable competitor wherever outright horsepower was not a decisive factor. On the other hand, a colossally expensive entry of two Group 2 cars in the Safari (part sponsored by Sears Roebuck) was a disappointment. Stig Blomqvist, plagued by transmission problems, trailed home in 13th place, while at the last minute Tom Trana could not start due to illness, and was replaced by one of Saab's ace mechanics, Berndt Melin, who finished a very creditable 18th.

With funds presumably quite low, little was then heard from Saab until the 1000 Lakes in Finland, where success was considered likely, if not certain. Stig Blomqvist and Per Eklund both started in twin 'cross-over'-Weber-engined V4s (fuel injection no longer seemed to figure on the engines of the factory cars). Stig was up to fourth place before the half-way halt, then in the second part of the event Stig overhauled his rivals and won the event, chalking up the first victory by a non-Finn in this very specialised Finnish rally.

Amazingly, Saab then sent the two driving stars – Blomqvist and Orrenius – to drive V4s in the non-Championship Portuguese TAP rally in October, which was always likely to be an uphill struggle against the Alpine-Renault and Lancias. Orrenius' final drive differential broke up in the first few hours, while Blomqvist's car broke a wheel following a puncture, and eventually ran out of time. An expensive folly, this one.

Finally came the all-special-stage event British RAC rally, where Saab had an excellent record. By this time, the 'works' cars had reached what would be their ultimate specification, with 1.8 litres and about 155bhp, and three of them – for Blomqvist, Eklund and Orrenius – turned up at the start in Harrogate. With 77 special stages scheduled for a five-day event, this was going to be a gruelling test.

As it happened, the wintry weather over much of the route – and particularly in Yorkshire, Keilder and Scotland where blizzards blocked some sections – could not have been better for Saab. Right from the start, the intrepid

Stig Blomqvist put in a blistering display of Saab V4 driving to win the British RAC rally in 1971. This was one of the Forestry Commission stages which made up most of the competitive mileage.

Blomqvist took the lead, and after a great deal of skilled and downright brave driving, held it all the way to the end.

At half distance, when the survivors struggled back into Harrogate, Stig led, Orrenius' car was fourth, and Eklund sixth – this was an extremely encouraging start. After that, not only did all three cars survive well, all the way to the end, but Stig won, Orrenius took third place, Per Eklund seventh, and the cars won the much coveted Manufacturers' Team Prize. Not only that, but in what had been a very 'thin' year, Saab took second place in the World Championship for Makes.

The long goodbye

Amazingly, the Saab V4's front-line rally career still had five years to evolve. However, changes in that time would be minimal – the team was stuck with its 1.8-litre V4 engines, and front-wheel-drive. In that time they would take on new livery, but no more performance, or any more reliability. Significantly, the new-generation 99 (later with a turbocharged engine) was on sale throughout the decade, and would eventually replace the V4.

Through those years Saab operated only a very limited programme. The stats tell their own story, as Saab took points on only 16 occasions in five years, this including just four victories.

1972

Highlights of the 1972 season included victory in the Swedish and 1000 Lakes, and second on the RAC – all events in which Saab traditionally did well. The Swedish was snow-covered, fast, specialised, and dominated by local heroes Stig Blomqvist, Carl Orrenius and Per Eklund. Stig's car set many fastest stage times on the 36-stage event, amazingly being competitive with Bjorn Waldegård's Porsche 911S, and finally won the event by more than two minutes. Just to rub it in, Stig then won the Finnish Hankiralli, which followed two weeks later.

Having abandoned the Safari as being too costly and too far from home, and having sent two cars to the Acropolis in Greece instead, where both suffered transmission problems, there was no more activity until August, whereupon the factory team entered Blomqvist in the Finnish 1000 Lakes,

On certain ice-covered special stages, Saab found that the best way to go quickly was to use the narrowest possible tyres, with the most sophisticated of treads and studs. Stig Blomqvist shows how, on the 1972 Swedish rally.

Driving a car which had been prepared by the 'satellite' competitions department in Finland, Simo Lampinen won the 1972 1000 Lakes in this 165bhp V4.

and supported Simo Lampinen, both in Group 5 cars (which were mechanically familiar except for modified cylinder heads, and had been lightened by almost 170lb/77kg), while Per Eklund had a normal Group 2 example.

The big battle was between these two Saabs and Timo Makinen's 2-litre-engined Ford Escort RS1600, but once the 240bhp Ford had suffered broken engine mountings, and Blomqvist had picked up an open-road speeding fine (his car later suffered from a blown engine), it was Lampinen who took the lead and held it to the end. After that, Eklund's third place in the Austrian Alpine was something of a sideshow, for all of Saab's late autumn attention was focused on the British RAC rally.

Based for the first time on the city of York, the RAC promised 72 special stages, for which Saab sent three new 1.8-litre V4s. Because Stig Blomqvist had won the event in 1971, he started as firm favourite, with the fiercest opposition likely to come from Ford's latest Escorts, two of which were fitted with the new 2-litre BDG engines. Yet, as rallying pundit John Davenport later wrote:

"The hypnotic ease with which Stig Blomqvist has won the past two Swedish rallies, the 1971 1000 Lakes and RAC rallies, led one to think that the combination of Blomqvist and Saab V4 was unbeatable if nothing went wrong ... in last year's snow, no Escort however well driven was going to get to grips with the Saab, and this year without snow it was equally clear that the reverse was true ..."

Written after the event, this reflected the fact that Roger Clark's Escort beat Blomqvist's Saab by nearly three-and-a-half minutes – but it did not reflect just what a titanic battle had run on and on for five days. After only one night, three of the four 'works' Escorts had retired, but Roger Clark held the lead from Blomqvist, with Per Eklund's Saab in third place. The gap was only 93 seconds at the halfway halt in York, for the two protagonists had already swopped many fastest stage times, and the battle continued for two more days after that. This event, too, was full of 'ifs,' for if Clark's late front suspension problem had not occurred on an easy road section before the finish (a front wheel bearing failed catastrophically), and if factory mechanics were not quickly to hand, he might have incurred road penalties having it mended, which would have handed victory to Blomqvist ...

Maybe we missed the fact that these outwardly staid-looking cars continued to evolve. As John Davenport reminded us in his annual *Autosport* survey:

"The title of the oldest car in rallying really belongs to the Saab 96, but that is a bit unfair on a design which has now swallowed a V4 engine, a couple of large Weber carburettors, various gearbox and suspension modifications and several styling changes since the start of the last decade ..."

1973

Another season, another modest programme, with just the one major outright victory – Sweden, of course – to add to the achievements board. This was the year in which an official FIA World Rally Championship was held, yet Saab barely figured.

Two factory-prepared cars, driven by Stig Blomqvist and Per Eklund, set up an incredible performance in Sweden in February, where there was lots of snow and ice, but where (for the organisers' own 'political' reasons) the use of studded tyres was completely banned. Saab, therefore, used the narrowest wheels and tyres it could find, and relied on its star drivers' unearthly skills to do the rest.

The fact is that the Saabs coped better than any other car or driver, and that Stig took a well-deserved victory, with team-mate Eklund second overall. Out of 36 special stages, Blomqvist was fastest on no fewer than 24 occasions and Eklund four times, which proved, once and for all, just how good the local car could be in local conditions.

This, though, was the highlight of the season, for a Saab would not score any more points until the 1000 Lakes in August (Saab chose to ignore rough and tough events like the Safari, Morocco and the Acropolis along the way).

For Saab, the 1000 Lakes was a huge disappointment. Stig Blomqvist's car led the event until three-quarter distance before his engine let go – and this was against 240bhp Ford Escorts, Porsches and similar very fast machines. In the end Simo Lampinen's car survived, and had to settle for fourth place, behind an Escort RS, a Volvo 142 (Markku Alen), and a Porsche 911 Carrera RS.

Once again Saab entered the (non-Championship) Austrian Alpine, and once again a broken transmission (on Blomqvist's car) let the side down, though he had been leading the event at the time. Saab's consolation was that although Bernard Darniche's Alpine-Renault A110 won the event, Per Eklund's Saab V4 finished second. Stig's car seemed to have an indestructible body shell, for having competed in the 1000 Lakes and in Austria, it then went on to Cyprus, where it won the rough-and-tough Cyprus rally quite comfortably.

Finally, there was the usual multi-car assault on the RAC rally in November, where Saab sent four cars, for Stig Blomqvist, Per Eklund, Simo Lampinen and (with help from Saab-Finland) Tapio Rainio. These machines were in their ultimate homologated specification, with perhaps 175bhp, much milder than hoped for, which meant that the Saabs were always struggling to match their rivals on straight-line performance. Even so, after the first day the remarkable Stig Blomqvist lay third, behind two Ford Escort RS1600s, though soon after this his car hit a rock while he was 'ditch-hooking' and damaged the suspension too much for it to continue. By the half-way halt, therefore, Lampinen was fifth and Eklund sixth, but the gaps were increasing. In the second leg, unhappily, both cars wilted, Lampinen's with a comprehensively trashed engine following persistent cooling water leaks.

1974

As far as motorsport was concerned, the winter of 1973/1974 was blighted by the Energy Crisis that gripped the world as a consequence of oil shortages following the Suez War. Rally after rally was cancelled, motorsport was completely banned for a time in certain countries, and after some normality had been restored at World level, Saab found little to do, would score points only in the second half of the year, and was without a victory.

During the winter, and looking for something – anything – to do, Saab entered the entire regular team in the Arctic rally, of Finland, which was a completely specialised snow rally. This was ideal for the Saabs, the result being that Tapio Rainio won the event, Stig Blomqvist was second, Simo Lampinen was fifth and Per Eklund sixth – a fine start to the season.

It was then months before the team actually took part in a World Championship rally, this being the Finnish 1000 Lakes in August. On a summer event where the stages were all very fast indeed, the V4s were always going to struggle against the likes of Hannu Mikkola and Timo Makinen in 2-litre Ford Escorts – and struggle they did. In the end fourth (Blomqvist) and fifth (Lampinen) was the best Saab could achieve.

Blomqvist was not, however, likely to give up without a big struggle. On the end-of-season RAC rally, where he and Per Eklund appeared in the now-familiar orange team V4s,

In 1973, the KAK organisers decided to ban the use of studded tyres in the Swedish International rally. This discouraged many cars from entering, but Saab merely treated it as a development exercise, and used ultra-narrow snow tyres. Stig Blomqvist (this car) won the event, and team-mate Per Eklund was second.

for in homologated guise they would never improve on the 1.8-litre engines now being used. As far as the spectators were concerned, the big difference was that the 'works' cars were now painted orange, rather than the blood-red which had been normal for more than a decade.

Praying for wet and snowy weather, this formidable team set out from York, determined to beat Ford, Lancia and the rest of rallying's world, but, unhappily, the weather was

Sometimes it didn't all end well – this was what was left of Per Eklund's V4 after the 1974 1000 Lakes rally.

he fought head-to-head with Timo Makinen's Ford Escort RS1600 and Sandro Munari's Lancia Stratos, eventually taking second place, just 1 minute 40 seconds off the pace. Sounds like a comfortable gap? Maybe, but one should remember that Stig rolled his car on an early stage in Wales, losing four minutes in the process. For the balance of the 84-stage event, spectators were thrilled to see Stig recovering, saw the car gradually become straighter and straighter, and saw the V4 set a series of fastest stage times. So, perhaps Makinen drove the more powerful Escort no faster than he needed to do ... but for Stig it was still a great performance. But what happened to Eklund's car? Per rolled it in Keilder, losing 12 minutes, and the hard-done-by car then shed a driveshaft a few hours later, stranding the driver.

1975

By 1975 Saab had run out of ways to make the dear old V4 any faster, and was turning its attention to the bigger (and potentially much faster) 99 model to secure its future. In 1975, therefore, Saab indulged itself, mainly in Scandinavia, to prove that the old cars were still competitive at times. In fact, Saab scored World Championship points just twice – in the Swedish, and in the Finnish 1000 Lakes.

After ignoring the Monte, where Lancia's Stratos was

In 1975 Saab signalled the arrival of a new generation of rally car, by posing the all-new 99 alongside one of the last of the V4s. Left-to-right: Stig Blomqvist, Erik Carlsson and Per Eklund.

forecast to win (which it did ...), Saab entered V4s for the Arctic rally, where deep snow was an ideal way to cut the opposition down to size. In a great performance, Simo Lampinen's Finnish-built car won the event, from Stig Blomqvist's Swedish-built car, with Jari Vilkas' Finnish-built example in third place. The Swedish and the Finnish operations made it their policy to co-operate, rather than to compete, the result being a real triumph, which reaped lots of publicity in Scandinavia.

Two 'works' cars, for Blomqvist and Eklund, were quick,

Per Eklund, sideways, in the Swedish rally of 1975. The V4 was always well-balanced for snow-and-ice events.

This is the Swedish rally of 1975, where one of the famous Lancia Stratos cars is leading a race around an ice-covered trotting track. There are two 'works' Saab V4s in the snow cloud behind!

but not quick enough, for the Swedish rally, which was as usual held in lots of snow and ice. Stig Blomqvist might have won the event if he had not been faced with the formidable combination of Bjorn Waldegård and a Lancia Stratos – and Per Eklund finished fourth. Stig, in fact, would have won the event if his V4's engine had not died with electrical failure on the start line of a test on an ice-covered trotting track in Karlstad, where a helpful push to the end of the stage (by Per Eklund) resulted in a heavy penalty being levied. Simo Lampinen then ended a most satisfactory month for Saab by winning the Finnish Hankiralli in his Finnish-built V4. After this, the team started to use the new 99 model in a variety of European events, and the venerable V4s would not appear once again until the 1000 Lakes in August.

The wait was, of course, worthwhile, for on the 1000 Lakes the team produced a real end-of-programme melange of models – two Swedish-built, two Finnish-built, one each with fuel injection. The Swedish cars ran in a pale green colour scheme – clearly there had been plenty of time to think about this outing, which was sure to be their last 'works' outing

Is there really a way through, between those railings? Stig Blomqvist's V4 on the 1000 Lakes rally of 1975.

in Scandinavia. As it happened, all cars were outpaced on this unique occasion by the amazing Hannu Mikkola/Toyota Corolla combination, but Simo took second place and Per Eklund fourth: as to Stig Blomqvist – he was disqualified at half-distance after picking up an open-road speeding ticket.

The end of the season, and Saab's traditional assault on the 72-stage British RAC rally, was an anti-climax, for although Blomqvist and Eklund arrived to compete in ultimate-specification machines, neither car made it to the finish. Eklund's car failed on the first day, Blomqvist rolled in the Clipstone complex, and his fuel-injected 1.9-litre engine's crankshaft later broke in a test in the Lake District. It was a sad end to this car's great career in the British rally.

1976

Amazingly, Saab still found life in its ancient car. Although 1976 would be the last season for the 'works' cars, Saab still managed a final victory (Sweden), and a good placing in the 1000 Lakes. After that, though, it really was all over, for the new-generation 99 then took over.

Above & right: Per Eklund's outright win in the 1976 Swedish rally was all the more remarkable because he beat team-mate Stig Blomqvist in a straight fight. That car is preserved in the Saab museum in Trollhättan.

After Tapio Rainio won the Arctic rally in a Finnish-built car (I almost said 'as usual,' for this sort of event was meat-and-drink to the Saab fraternity), and just before he repeated that trick on the Hankiralli, the Swedish factory entered its two contracted drivers – Stig Blomqvist and Per Eklund – in the Swedish rally, their home event where they could always expect to be competitive.

A famous victory – when Per Eklund (right) and Bjorn Cederberg won the 1976 KAK Swedish rally, narrowly defeating their team-mate, Stig Blomqvist.

And so it was. Even though they faced formidable opposition from Bjorn Waldegård, Walfridsson and Lampinen in mid-engined Lancia Stratos types, the V4s were just as dominant on snow as usual, especially as the Swedish organisers were once again allowing studded tyres to be used. A look down the 34 special stage times tells us that one or other of the Saabs was fastest on no fewer than 30 occasions. There appeared to be no team orders, the team-mates were rivals but bitterly so throughout, and at the end of the event, the only surprise was that Eklund won the event, with Stig Blomqvist second, though the gap was a mere 96 seconds.

With months then to hang about, tackling local Scandinavian events, was it even worth waiting for the 1000 Lakes, where Escorts, Fiat 131 Abarths and Stratos monsters might outstrip the factory V4s? On reflection, maybe it was not, for the cars were truly outpaced. Saab hedged its bets

Per Eklund won the KAK Swedish rally in 1976, a fine performance by the V4 when it was coming to the end of its career.

Driving the winner

Only days after Simo Lampinen won the RAC rally of 1968, Saab GB invited *Autocar's* Martin Lewis to spend a day in the car, on a quasi special stage not far from London. As the car was driven not more than a week after the famous victory, there had been little time for re-preparation.

With permission from *Autocar*, some extracts from this test are illuminating:

'The RAC-winning car is tuned to Group 2: This means reworked cylinder heads, special manifolds and a fat twin-choke Weber, which drinks fuel at the rate of about 15mpg ...

'In the boot, the big 12-gallon fuel tank takes up a lot of room: but there is still space for two spare wheels, a stand-by fuel can, and a rack of various BP oils ...

'One's first impression from the driving seat is that the Saab is not a special. Neatness abounds, even to the way that the engine just came to life without any fuss or bother ...

'But, let loose on the roads for which it was designed, the Saab is in its element. Although the front wheels do the work, it is not in that urgent, Super Mouse, way of the Cooper S: it is more like a Land-Rover, with 15in. wheels shod in great lumps of Dunlop rubber, biting into earth. The traction is little short of amazing and the Saab would just walk away from the thickest mud we happened to stop in ...

'Off slowly, at first, to get the feel. Bottom gear is high, and nothing much happens until the needle is past the 3,000rpm mark. Then things go made, with lumps of mud flying up as you get wheel-spin. The steering column gear change is excellent, with a light, precise, action needing just a wrist flick between ratios. One gets the impression of great solidity – that great ditch is crossed with just a grate from the sump shield, and on straights the revs go storming up to the red line. A flick into third – wipers on for that puddle – and then down to second for the "bomb hole" ...

'Suspension movements on the Saab are long and this helps the car keep its balance on rough stuff. It takes a really big "yump" to put the wheels off the ground, so one rarely seems to lose all contact. I think that the best "pat on the back" one can give the Saab is for the way it stood up to our driving. Not perhaps as hard as Mr Lampinen, yet what we did to that car was not very pleasant. After three hours of special stage driving – and this included several unplanned excursions into the outback, hundreds of spin-jarring passes through our favourite puddle and probably quite a few unnecessary thumps on the sump shield, Ol' No.19 just stood in the sun and steamed happily at us, covered in Hampshire mud ...'

by entering Blomqvist and Eklund in 99s, so it was the two white-and-blue Saab-Finland V4s that tried so hard on the super-fast and flowing stages. Lampinen and Rainio did the driving, but both cars were known to be in transmission trouble, so Simo settled for a 1.8-litre rather than a 1.9-litre engine and hoped for the best.

At the half-way point, Rainio was fifth and Lampinen sixth, but shortly thereafter Rainio's car suffered from failing rear brakes and lost eight minutes on the road. Even for Simo, though, bravery was not enough, as his V4 took fifth place, a long way off the pace. Time and technology had finally caught up with the Saabs, for each of the four cars which beat Simo had 16-valve engines, perhaps 240bhp, and rear-wheel-drive.

With 99s now being preferred by the Swedish team drivers and (for publicity reasons) by top management, that

Even at the very end of its run, the V4 was still used as a rally car. The occasion is the 1980 RAC rally, and these are the 'works' cars supported by Clarion. Stig Blomqvist (right) and Ola Stromberg (centre) are in 99 Turbos, while Kalle Grundel (left) is in a V4. There was no luck on that occasion.

really was the end of the World Championship road for the V4s. Thereafter they would be seen only at European level, in rallycross, or in the hands of private owners, looked on fondly by thousands of enthusiasts, but no longer guaranteed winners.

Past its best? What rivals took over?

If the truth be told, as a rally car the front-wheel-drive V4

One of the V4's final victories came in the Hankiralli of early 1977. After that the team would concentrate on 99 development.

Per Eklund gives his 'works' V4 the high-jump treatment in a Swedish rallycross event in the 1970s.

was well-and-truly obsolete before Saab finally retired it as a front-line rally car in 1976. In 1.8-litre form, complete with twin-choke Weber carburettors, there was a short time when it had been tenuously competitive in the early 1970s, after which two types of modern rally car – the rear-engine (911/Alpine-Renault breed) – began to overtake it on gravel, while the ultra-powerful 'specials' – Ford Escort RS, Lancia Stratos and Fiat Abarth 131 – became more effective on tarmac. As I have already made clear, the V4 was never competitive on tarmac, and its last clear victory on gravel had come in 1972 (1000 Lakes), after which it could only occasionally win on ultra-low-friction events, such as the Swedish or lesser Scandinavian events, where surfaces were usually hard-packed snow and ice, and where the drivers' expertise, particularly in choosing the right tyres, could balance other shortcomings.

Although Saab tried to replace the V4 with the 99 and 99 Turbo (as explained below), and had some success with those bulky machines, the days of front-wheel-drive supremacy were now over.

How could Saab replace the V4?

By the early 1970s – indeed, several years before the last of the 'works' V4s was built – it was clear that the limits of their performance had been reached. Wherever rally regulations allowed, and the cars could run outside the limits of homologation, they used 1.8-litre or even 1.9-litre engines with up to 175bhp, but except on extremely slippery surfaces where traction was an issue, this was no longer enough to match up to cars like the rear-engined Alpine-Renaults and Porsches, the purpose-built mid-engined Lancia Stratos, or the conventional (front-engine/rear-drive) Ford Escort RS1600. In any case, for the last few years, the most powerful of V4 Saabs was always likely to damage its front-wheel-drive transmission, and there was nothing within the bounds of homologation regulations, that could be done about that.

In an ideal world, and with a big budget, Saab would have turned to a new generation of super-compact car which delivered more power, without a weight penalty, but in the real world, in its range, and with only modest motorsport budgets available, this was not feasible. Saab was simply not able to spend the same sort of money as Ford, Fiat or Lancia and, whether one liked to admit it or not, money equalled power ...

Saab's only alternative was to develop the larger and more modern Saab 99, which had been in production since 1969. Although this retained all the expected Saab virtues – it had front-wheel-drive, and was extremely strong – the 99 had never been intended as a dedicated competition car, and at that stage still had only a 110bhp/2-litre single overhead camshaft engine: unhappily it weighed a discouragingly high 2400lb/1090kg.

It started its first rally – the Nordland, in the north of Germany, close to the Danish border – in May 1975, and won its first rally (the Boucles de Spa, in Belgium, in 99EMS form) in February 1976.

Although things looked up in 1977 with the arrival of the 145bhp/2-litre turbocharged version (the 99 Turbo), this was still a car which was too heavy and – worse – it had never been conceived as an 'homologation special.' At a time when Fiat's 131 Abarth, Ford's Escort RS1800, and Lancia's Stratos were all purpose-built competition cars, Saab found it difficult to cope – it simply did not have the budget or the resources to match the 'big boys' – so as the 1980s dawned, Saab wisely and gracefully withdrew from the sport at world level, but was much missed.

The larger 99 model took over from the V4, in motorsport, in the late 1970s. This was a Finnish-prepared car in the snows of Sweden.

World/major European rally wins

Note: Original cars surveyed here were Saab 96s, with 841cc two-stroke engines. Later cars had different sub-model names, as listed. Saab V4s went into production in 1966, and used four-stroke Ford-Germany V4 engines.

Event	Car	Drivers
1960		
Midnight Sun	P9293	Carl-Magnus Skogh/Rolf Skogh
1000 Lakes	AR900	Carl-Otto Bremer/Juhania Lampi
Viking	P9293	Carl-Magnus Skogh/Rolf Skogh
RAC	P80351	Erik Carlsson/Stuart Turner
1961		
Acropolis	P9315	Erik Carlsson/Walter Karlsson
Midnight Sun	P49307	Carl-Magnus Skogh/Rolf Skogh
RAC	P8680	Erik Carlsson/John Brown
1962		
Monte Carlo	P614444	Erik Carlsson/Gunnar Haggbom
RAC	P91990	Erik Carlsson/David Stone
1963		
Monte Carlo	P77558	Erik Carlsson/Gunnar Palm
1000 Lakes	Not identified	Simo Lampinen/Jyrki Ahava
1964		
Flowers (San Remo)	P44301	Erik Carlsson/Gunnar Palm
1000 Lakes	Not identified	Simo Lampinen/Jyrki Ahava
1966		
Swedish	P44302	Åke Andersson/Sven-Olof Svedberg

Event	Car	Drivers
From this time, all victories were achieved with Saab V4s		
1967		
Czech	PA8935	Erik Carlsson/Torsten Aman
1968		
RAC	PA9782	Simo Lampinen/John Davenport
Second in the World Championship for Makes		
1969		
Scottish	PA8523	Simo Lampinen/Arne Hertz
1970		
Fourth in the World Championship for Makes		
1971		
Swedish	PA55658	Stig Blomqvist/Arne Hertz
1000 Lakes	PA55658	Stig Blomqvist/Arne Hertz
RAC	PA57003	Stig Blomqvist/Arne Hertz
Second in the World Championship for Makes		
1972		
Swedish	PA57007	Stig Blomqvist/Arne Hertz
1000 Lakes	A1361	Simo Lampinen/Klaus Sohlberg
Fifth in the World Championship for Makes		
1973		
Swedish	PA57014	Stig Blomqvist/Arne Hertz
Fifth in the World Championship for Makes		
1976		
Arctic (Hanki)	AEC 501	Tapio Rainio/Erkki Nyman
Swedish	ETK 909	Per Eklund/Bjorn Cederberg
Fourth in the World Championship for Makes		

More great rally books from Veloce:

ISBN 978-1-845849-94-8

ISBN 978-1-787113-30-5

RALLY

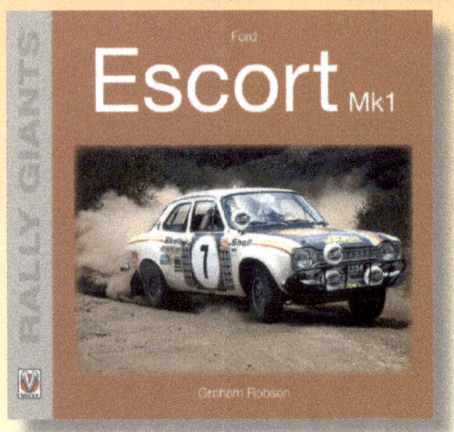

ISBN 978-1-787111-07-3

ISBN 978-1-787113-25-1

ISBN 978-1-787113-24-4

ISBN 978-1-845841-83-6

ISBN 978-1-787111-09-7

ISBN 978-1-845842-58-1

www.veloce.co.uk

* Prices subject to change • P&P extra

GIANTS

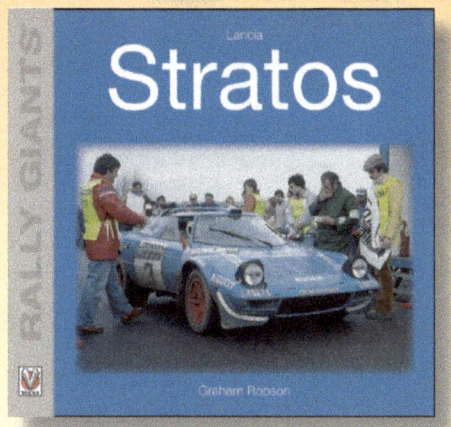
ISBN 978-1-787111-08-0

ISBN 978-1-84584-141-6

ISBN 978-1-787113-22-0

978-1-787111-71-4

ISBN 978-1-787113-31-2

ISBN 978-1-787111-11-0

www.veloce.co.uk

* Prices subject to change • P&P extra

More great rally books from Veloce:

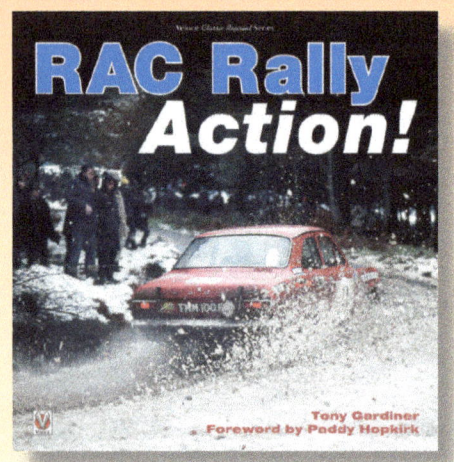

ISBN 978-1-787112-29-2

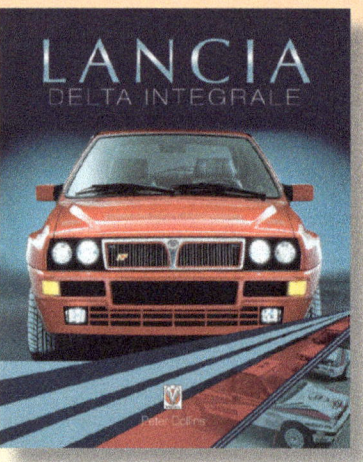

ISBN 978-1-787110-76-2

ISBN 978-1-787111-28-8

ISBN 978-1-787112-28-5

ISBN 978-1-845848-70-5

ISBN 978-1-84584-208-6

Index

Aaltonen, Rauno 61, 79, 80, 83
Alen, Markku 108
Alpine-Renault (& models) 12, 15, 93, 101, 104, 108, 119
Andersson, Gunnar 12, 57, 61
Antao, Seraphino 69
Audi (& models) 51, 52, 54
Austin (and BMC models) 19, 48, 50
Austin-Healey (& models) 13, 48, 65, 67, 70, 79, 80, 83
Autocar 20, 55, 117
Autosport 30, 31, 59, 85, 108
Auto Union (& models) 41, 55

Bengtsson, Gunnar 55
Bengtsson, Harry 65
BMC (& models) 63
Bohringer, Eugen 61, 63, 65, 67, 70, 80, 81
Bolster, John 31
British Leyland (& models) 94
Bullough, Jimmy 94

Citroen (& models) 59, 65, 67
Clark, Jim 86
Clark, Roger 92, 97, 108
Clerk, Sir Dugald 26

Darniche, Bernard 108
Davenport, John 34, 85, 86, 89, 107, 108
DKW (& models) 10, 11, 15, 17, 18, 26, 41, 65, 78

Elford, Vic 12, 65, 80, 94
European Rally Championship 12, 47, 65, 67, 70
European Rallycross Championship 54

Fiat (& models) 51, 116, 119, 120

Ford (& models) 12, 14, 15, 27, 32, 34, 40, 48, 51, 67, 70, 74, 75, 77, 80, 86, 89, 92-94, 97, 98, 101, 107-110, 116, 119, 120

Gele, Pierre 65
Gott, John 30, 50, 59
Grorndahl, Robbie 44

Harper, Peter 63
Hellberg, Bo 25, 41, 43-45, 89, 103
Hopkirk, Paddy 48, 67, 70
Hughes, Peter 74

Jansson, Bengt 70

Kallstrom, Harry 70, 97, 98

Lancia (& models) 12, 15, 49, 51, 70, 89, 94, 95, 97, 98, 100, 101, 104, 109, 110, 113, 116, 119, 120
Lewis, Martin 117
Ljungfeldt, Bo 67, 70

Mabbs, Geoff 61
Makinen, Timo 80, 81, 83, 89, 94, 98, 107, 109, 110
McQueen, Steve 98
Melde, Rolf 17
Melin, Berndt 104
Mercedes-Benz (& models) 55, 59, 61, 63, 65, 67, 70, 80
Mikkola, Hannu 93, 97, 109, 114
Mini, Mini-Cooper (& models) 10-12, 14, 15, 20, 27, 31, 32, 41, 48, 65, 67, 70, 80, 81, 83, 85, 86, 89
Morris (& models) 19, 48
Moss, Stirling 48
Munari, Sandro 110

Nissan (& models) 51

Olsson, Sven 41
Oy Valmet AB 28, 43

Panhard (& models) 59, 61
Peugeot (& models) 51, 63
Pfenier, K 78
Plymouth Barracuda 85
Porsche (& models) 11, 12, 32, 55, 59, 61, 65, 70, 81, 88, 89, 92, 94, 97, 98, 100, 101, 106, 108, 119

Rallies:
  1000 Lakes (Finland) 36, 46, 47, 50, 51, 57, 61, 65, 80, 83, 86, 89, 93, 94, 98, 100, 101, 104, 106- 110, 113, 114, 116, 119
  Acropolis 12, 47, 50, 55, 59, 61, 65, 70, 80, 82, 83, 85, 86, 92, 97, 106, 108
  Alpine (Austrian) 86, 92, 94, 97, 100, 108
  Alpine (French) 30, 47, 61, 65, 77, 78, 80, 83, 85, 86, 89
  Arctic 104, 109, 111, 115
  Baja 1000 33, 35, 36, 98, 99, 101
  Boucles de Spa 120
  Cyprus 108
  Czech (Vltava) 83, 86, 88, 92, 97
  Danube 89
  (Rallye dei) Fiori/Flowers (Italy) 47, 70, 74, 86, 100
  Geneva 65, 80, 86
  German 47, 86
  Gulf London 86, 88, 92
  Hankiralli 101, 104, 106, 115, 117
  Liège-Rome-Liège (later Liège-Sofia-Liège, later Spa-Sofia-Liège) 30, 41, 47,

48, 61, 65, 70, 79, 80, 83
London-Mexico World Cup 100
London-Sydney Historic Marathon 52
London-Sydney Marathon 94
Lyon-Charbonnieres 86
Midnight Sun (Sweden) 44, 47, 50, 55, 56, 59-61, 65, 70, 76, 80, 81
Monte Carlo 12, 20, 41, 42, 45, 47, 59, 61, 63, 64, 67-73, 80, 81, 85, 86, 92, 110
Morocco 108
Nordland 120
Norway 57, 100, 101
Norwegian Winter 53
Polish 50, 59, 61, 65, 86, 89
Portugal (TAP) 47, 104
RAC 10, 31, 34, 44, 45, 47, 51, 52, 57, 58, 60-63, 65, 66, 70, 80, 83, 86, 89, 92-94, 98, 100, 101, 104-109, 114, 117, 118
Safari 12, 47, 64, 67, 69, 70, 75, 81, 85, 86, 104, 106, 108
San Remo – see Fiori/Flowers
Scottish 36, 92, 96, 97
Spanish 89
Swedish (KAK) 14, 40, 50, 51, 53, 54, 84, 86, 87, 90, 91, 92, 94, 95, 100-103, 106, 108-110, 112-116, 120
Three Cities 86
Tulip 19, 30, 50, 55, 59, 61, 63, 70, 78, 81, 85, 86, 87
Viking 50, 56
Renault (& models) 19
Rudh, Pelle 41

Saab models:
  90 Scandia passenger aircraft 15
  91 training aircraft 31
  92 and 92B model 9, 11, 16, 17, 18, 19, 20, 31, 46, 55
  93 and 93B model 10, 11, 16- 20, 31, 46, 50, 55
  95 Estate 20, 28, 31, 41, 59, 61
  98 (factory code name for 96 V4) 27
  99 model 28
  99 Turbo model 48, 51
  750GT 17, 20, 40
  B17 fighter aircraft 15
  Granturismo 850 20

'Monster' prototype 13
Sonett Super Sport 17, 31
Sonett II (Type 94) 40, 86
Sonett III (Type 97) 40
Saab premises and workshops:
  Trollhättan 15, 17, 29, 32, 41, 44, 45, 46
  Uusikaupunki (Finland) 28, 43
Saab race and rally drivers:
  Aman, Torsten 83, 85, 88, 98
  Andersson, Åke 43, 70, 80, 81, 83-86
  Andersson, Ove 43, 83
  Blomqvist, Stig 10, 11, 41, 43, 47, 51-54, 88, 94, 98, 100-106, 108-111, 113-118
  Bremer, Carl Otto 57
  Brown, John 63
  Carlsson, Erik 9-11, 20, 25, 28-30, 32, 33, 40-49, 51, 55, 57-72, 74-83, 85, 86, 88, 89, 98, 99, 101, 111
  Cederberg, Bjorn 51, 116
  Dahl, Olle 70, 83
  Davenport, John 34, 92, 93
  Domleo, Val 70, 74
  Eklund, Per 40, 47, 53, 54, 98, 100, 104-117, 119
  Grundel, Kalle 118
  Haggbom, Gunnar 63
  Hertz, Arne 52, 96, 103
  Jonsson, Lasse 86, 97
  Karlsson, Walter 55
  Lampinen, Simo 34, 36, 41, 43, 44, 50, 51, 65, 80, 83, 85, 86, 88, 89, 92-98, 100, 102, 107-109, 111, 113, 114, 116, 117
  Larsson, Jerry 83, 91, 92
  Lindberg, Hakan 89, 92, 98, 100
  Lindqvist, Ingvar 98
  Lund, Hans 83
  Molander, Greta 10, 11
  Moss, Pat 41, 43, 48, 49, 63, 70-72, 74, 77, 78, 80, 81, 83, 85-89, 101
  Moss, Stirling 81
  Nystrom, Liz 77
  Orrenius, Carl 34, 55, 85, 88, 89, 92, 94, 97, 98, 100, 104-106
  Palm, Gunnar 45, 67, 68, 72, 74, 76, 78-80
  Palm, Torsten 91, 102

Rainio, Tapio 44, 108, 115, 117
Skogh, Carl-Magnus 9-12, 46, 50, 55-57, 60, 61, 63, 65, 70
Skogh, Rolf 60
Stone, David 65, 66
Stromberg, Ola 118
Svedberg, Sven Olof 84
Trana, Tom 12, 34, 88, 90, 92, 94, 98, 100, 101, 104
Turner, Stuart 57, 58, 59, 63
Unnerud, John 100
Vilkas, Jari 111
Schock, Walter 55
Skoda (& models) 52
Skogh, Carl-Magnus 83
Soderstrom, Bengt 65
Sprinzel, John 67
Standard (& models) 17
Staepelaere, Gilbert 93
Sunbeam (& models) 63
Svenska Aeroplan AB 15
Swaner, Bo 28, 43, 45, 63, 103

Toivonen, Pauli 65, 67
Toyota (& models) 54, 114
Trana, Tom 70, 80, 81
Trautmann, René 59, 61
Triumph (& models) 50, 51, 54, 61, 80

Vauxhall 14
Vinatier, Jean 93
Volvo (& models) 11, 12, 15, 50, 55, 57, 61, 70, 80-83, 86, 108
VW (& models) 11, 63, 70

Waldegård, Bjorn 12, 92, 97, 100, 101, 106, 113, 116
Walfridsson, Per 116
Walter, Hans 61, 65
World Rally Championship 51, 101, 105, 108-110

Zasada, Sobieslaw 88

www.ingramcontent.com/pod-product-compliance
Lightning Source LLC
Chambersburg PA
CBHW040930240426
43672CB00021B/2994